WHAT WENT WRONG, OR WAS IT RIGHT?

JACKSON PHILLIPS III

authorHOUSE®

AuthorHouse™
1663 Liberty Drive
Bloomington, IN 47403
www.authorhouse.com
Phone: 1 (800) 839-8640

Published by AuthorHouse 01/14/2019

ISBN: 978-1-5462-7584-8 (sc)
ISBN: 978-1-5462-7583-1 (hc)
ISBN: 978-1-5462-7582-4 (e)

Library of Congress Control Number: 2019900403

CHAPTER 1

DISCOVERY AND QUESTIONS

Tuesday, August 12, 2095

Dear Andrew,

First, thanks a lot for all your hard work in the farmhouse attic this weekend. You and I made real good progress until we found that old trunk full of my father's stuff. Guess he would be your great-great-grandfather. His collection of magazine clippings from around the turn of the century is amazing. It was fun looking back at what life was like that long ago, and I will have a much more detailed look. There will be plenty of time to finish the attic cleanup later. You had many questions, and I didn't do a great job of answering them and explaining things. I was just a kid myself at the time of all this, and I was not very interested in politics, government, etc. But you really surprised me in the way you phrased your last question. Remember? You asked, "What went wrong?" Guess I had always thought things had progressed very well since that time when many things were so troubled.

So, your question whets my appetite to do more research. At the time you asked the "What went wrong?" question, I believe we both were feeling surprised at just how much had changed in all facets of life in America—and of course the world also. We first noticed, in the media used for communication then, the vast array of products and services being advertised. Lifestyle choices were so broad. Then we were surprised at all the controversies, scandals, crimes, safety issues, and fighting that

1

seemed to be prevalent almost a century ago. We had a chance to talk awhile about how different our lives are today. Besides the security issues, we agreed the living and working situations have changed dramatically as well. On reflection, it seems to me that our lives, although so much more secure now, are a lot more restricted than in those days. I still can't agree that the right question to ask is, "What went wrong?" but I concede your point that, on balance, the changes were probably not all good.

Well, as you know, I will hit one hundred in about fifteen months and will move to the farm, and it is not likely we will have any time together after that. So, I'm going to do some research now and will set down in some communiqués to you what I learn about some of the big changes that have happened since the start of our century and also see what I can figure out about why they happened. I hope you will do some research there as time allows, *but don't neglect your studies.* On your trips home, as you complete terms at the university, I hope you will have time to discuss some of this with me.

Love,
Your *great*-grandfather, Pops

CHAPTER 2

THE BIG PICTURE

Dear Andrew,

Thanks for your thoughts and encouragement on this. I appreciate your offer of help, but don't ease up on your studies.

Before I get too deep into this research, I have thought some about how to manage our investigation. Some of this century's changes are readily apparent by comparing the old way against all the improvements in our current everyday life. Significant changes were responses to huge problems in my father's era. We think little about them now because these dilemmas were approached and resolved so long ago. It should be most interesting to see how these problems were solved, particularly since my father seems to have been somehow involved in determining the fixes.

I know you are very busy at the university, but I would appreciate it if you could look for coverage gaps or omissions in the subject areas I will try to cover. I'm surprised that in the literature I've surveyed so far there is very little discussion of the changes in life and lifestyle since the turn of the century and the time these documents were produced. In fact, there seems to be very light treatment and even major gaps or omissions from this period compared to all the facts in the historical literature of the early years of our nation.

This job will be harder than I thought, but here goes on my first thoughts.

TODAY COMPARED TO CIRCA 1980–2020

Relative to those days, we are very healthy now with longer life spans and little sickness. We have our daily pills; I take the usual red, white, and blue caplets plus a fourth one that is speckled brown. These seem to take good care of our health. The daily monitor check on the home communications kiosk quickly determines if something in our system, including our psyche, is going wrong. Our monitor persons (MPs) report any abnormalities instantly, and alerted health authorities are quick to determine the fix needed. This is so different from the old days. Near the turn of this century, there were thousands of hospitals and several million doctors. Still, contagions, pollution, poor health-care practices, and misuse of drugs everywhere caused or prolonged all kinds of weird, painful, and deadly diseases. Physical injuries are much less frequent now because of better facilities and safety practices. This country's progress on health since those days has been amazing.

I know, of course, that we older folks usually die pretty quickly once we move to the farms—the townships set up for us. I agree with this practice, although as I approach the maximum age of one hundred, it is hard not to have misgivings. Guess I'm lucky to not be in the group of folks who go early because they run out of finances before one hundred. Study hard, and implement your career plans carefully, or you could be among those who must go even sooner. Anyway, I'll be at the farm next year after my birthday. This current research will liven up my life for a while, and as you know, I believe in an afterlife where we can all meet again.

Transportation—one of your big interests, if not yet your major—has seen very dramatic changes. But you may not have investigated its history. For example, in the old days, most people used private automobiles. They really weren't very *automatic* either. You had to drive the vehicle yourself. There were lots of wrecks, resulting in bad injuries and fatalities. The large number of private cars and commercial trucks for freight caused bad air pollution as well. Most of these vehicles were powered by petroleum-based liquid fuels, like the racing cars and some of our off-system sports cars of today. They were a far cry from the government-provided, self-guided electrics now available everywhere for our use. There were a few primitive trains run by private companies in the US. Many other countries had already made large technical strides in train technology and had high citizen usage of trains. There were many airplanes, including smaller ones you could fly yourself. These private planes and all the commercial aircraft were powered by some form of petrol and were slow and dangerous.

Careers were much more complicated then. Job progression was variable, and advancement was not necessarily based on merit. Financial security was uncertain as well. There were ups and downs in job availability and income depending on your company's success and what they called "business cycles." Manufacturing and other businesses were mostly private, operating with very little mutual cooperation and, in many cases, severe competition between them. Education, career development, and job training were not carefully monitored or controlled. It appears much talent was wasted. Salaries and savings seemed more variable then, and retirement resources were far from secure. The US government was run by elected officials and career professionals like today, but it had far fewer employees. The politicians' main focus appeared to be getting reelected. The government tried to monitor industry practices and safety-related matters but without much success. A lot of attention seemed to be focused on the federal and state taxing aspects and on giving economic advantage to favored industries or companies.

Population change was not controlled. At the turn to this century, about one-third of the US population was basically in poverty. I also read that less than 10 percent of the population controlled over 90 percent of the wealth. Individual and group behavior across the wealth strata was quite variable. Crime was prevalent, both major and minor, resulting in physical harm and financial damage. Resources were not well controlled. There were cyclical shortages and a lot of waste of food and the other necessities of life. The quality of potable water was not well regulated, and many people suffered negative health consequences from ingesting low-quality water. Due to poor quality and planned obsolescence, product replacement was frequent, and many more services—like repairs and maintenance—were required. Food service operations like restaurants were diversified and overabundant but generally very expensive for what you got.

There were troubles between people based on race or country of origin. Population movement, including immigration, was poorly controlled.

There were significant troubles caused by the wide variation in resource ownership and the differences in social status.

Recreation and entertainment were extremely diversified, and much of it was dangerous to the body or the psyche. Illegal stimulants had widespread use, and both drug users and drug traffickers engendered a variety of violent crimes and unnecessary deaths. The human reproduction process was poorly controlled and was badly misused by many. Family life was very different and not secure. Often relatives even physically harmed each other. Communication and information technology were moving strongly into the electronic era, but the externalities didn't seem to stabilize until about 2025.

There is so much that has changed in the variety of things we call life. I admit that I am very excited about doing more research and expect it will help in resolving the difference in our views about whether the changes were good or bad.

There is another issue that is also becoming plain to me. Were all the specific changes necessary, or were they only the best answers then ascertainable for all the ills of that period?

Love, Pops

CHAPTER 3

TRAVEL AND TRANSPORTATION

Dear Andrew,

In general, transportation at the turn of the century was very important to the individual and to the economy, but it was both unsafe and very expensive.

Because of your special interests, you are well aware of just how many aspects of transportation changed in this century. In my early years the common vehicle for personal transportation was a four-wheeled automobile, or "car." They were very numerous. I remember my father owned an open vehicle with only two wheels similar to our motorized sporting cycles of today. Private-use vehicles as well as the commercial trucks used for the required movement of goods were powered by combustion of liquid petroleum products. This resulted in a lot of exhaust of byproduct gases, some quite harmful. Besides affecting the air people were breathing, the exhaust also was a major contributor to a change in air quality at the atmospheric level. Although at first this was disputed by some scientists, it was concluded that harmful exhaust constituents were causing a much-too-rapid rise in atmospheric temperature. The dangers from this became obvious to all, and changes were made. Back in those days only a few cars and public transportation systems used electricity or "natural" gas, the cleanest energy sources then available.

In the earlier times all electricity, including that generated at nuclear plants, was created by steam-based turbines. Most used coal and petroleum products to create the steam. This of course directly contributed to environmental damage. Electricity is now predominantly produced in nonpolluting ways, including the use of solar technology, direct-nuclear reactions, and cleaner-burning biofuels. Very effective stack gas scrubbers must now be used with fuel-burning operations. Government taxing and regulations have made the newer generating methods cheaper than all previous methods except for the few existing hydraulic dams.

Riverboats and ocean ships have been largely displaced from the transportation of people, except for pleasure cruises. They remain major goods transporters today, but some, particularly those with foreign ownership, still use liquid petroleum fuels instead of nuclear power. Such international oceangoing ships burn petroleum-based fuels, both diesel and the dirtier, bottom-of-the-barrel bunker fuel. "Bunkers" are lower priced, and earlier in the century ships that used such fuel were allowed to emit the resulting severe pollution from their smokestacks while on the open seas. Bunker fuel quality was improved some near the turn of the century, but the old form without smokestack cleanup remained legal on the open seas for a long time.

Trains, along with passenger ships, were for many years the major mode of transport for long-distance human travel after automobiles, but not so after the 1950s. Importantly, however, they continued to carry much of the cross-country freight. The locomotives that pulled the trains originally were coal fired but early in the twentieth century were switched to cleaner and more convenient diesel fuel made from petroleum. Today, of course, trains are again popular people transporters, and all our new high-speed trains are powered by electricity.

In the mid-twentieth century, airplanes started coming into more prominent use for passenger travel, and both trains and ships gradually became almost exclusively used to transport goods. Air transportation enhanced its position because of major improvements in the safety and convenience of flying passengers as well as freight. Our government has also done much to prevent highly publicized terrorist acts via airplanes as well as operational and control carelessness endangering air travel. They have also conquered the long security-related waits by using new technologies and procedures that are possible with the centralized, direct government control of the airline industry. There has been some progress in electric-powered planes as nuclear power plants have gotten smaller.

Automobiles, however, have seen the largest external change. The number of cars in the US was previously very close to the number of citizens above the minimum driving age. The personal vehicles had even become strong status symbols! Your automobile represented your interests as well as your financial status. So it took quite a variety of transportation devices to satisfy these needs. As a result, there were dozens of manufacturers and many, many models by each manufacturer. Accessories and expensive optional gadgets were continuously developed that also individualized cars and the then-popular small trucks. But increasing prices and rising fuel costs made such private transportation ever more costly to owners. Repairs and tuning were too often required, and recalls of defective products were frequent. Automobiles also became a very expensive proposition for the national interests, particularly as foreign car manufacturers became the dominant automotive companies. In addition, a lot of foreign petroleum was required to supply enough of the required fuels. Still, the automobile manufacturers and fuel-producing companies were the largest and most powerful industries in the US until electronic and communication technology companies began their heyday after the turn to the twenty-first century.

Automobiles, trucks, and motorcycles were also major killers and injurers during this time. Accidents were frequent and deadly, even though typical speed limits were thirty to forty-five miles per hour in busy metropolitan areas and fifty-five to seventy-five miles per hour on the dangerous and expensive-to-maintain roads and highways of the times. Wrecks, whether involving a single vehicle or multiple ones, almost always resulted in serious injuries. Motorcycle wrecks had an especially high risk for death and bad injuries. In fact, vehicle accidents killed over thirty-five thousand Americans each year and hospitalized countless others. In addition to road hazards, wrecks were caused by bad visibility, plain carelessness, and people "driving under the influence" of alcohol or drugs. Driver attention loss while using handheld communication devices also caused problems. "Road rage" incidents, where one driver got so upset by the actions of another that chases and direct confrontations ensued, were not unusual. Informal racing on public streets and highways was not uncommon either, particularly among young drivers. Car thefts resulted in many other kinds of major problems, with the stolen cars being subsequently used in a range of criminal activities—from kids going on joy rides to major theft rings stealing specific cars by type and quickly repainting or otherwise disguising the cars for resale. Cars and trucks of the day, particularly stolen ones, were also used in smuggling, principally of illegal drugs hidden in natural crevices of the automobile or in disguised containers. The vehicles were also used for transporting illegal immigrants, another problem of that day.

So personal and property safety was just as important a factor in transportation changes as the national reduction in expenditures for personal cars and the lowering of air pollution. Together, these problems provided lots of incentive for the subsequent great conversion to our new government-owned standard electrics. In addition to allowing for higher average speeds and reducing travel times, the automatic guidance systems we have today have almost eliminated traffic injuries and deaths from accidents. I'm not sure how many government electrics are available now, but there is always a surplus of ready-to-go vehicles at each station I use. Only a few models are needed now, just enough to efficiently handle the correct number of passengers and to provide the extra space needed for longer trips. I'm amazed at the estimates of the cost savings that have been realized by changing our national fleet, even without factoring in the many lives saved, the injuries prevented, and the health and atmospheric improvements because of substantially reduced pollution.

CHAPTER 4

MEDIA AND ENTERTAINMENT

Dear Andrew,

This should be an "entertaining" communiqué, covering the world of entertainment almost one hundred years ago and seeing how dramatically that has changed. The range and variety of choices offered to the population then is surprising. Entertainment was a very big part of the economy and almost totally uncontrolled, as far as I can see. At some point after the economic changes began, much of the entertainment was judged harmful to the general population and was put almost totally under government control. I would appreciate your view on whether this was right or wrong as a government action.

Compared to many parts of the entertainment world, the concert, opera, ballet, and stage productions existed pretty much as we have today, but now the themes are more carefully monitored. Many of the performance groups required financial support from government agencies and charities before the big changeover, but as far as I can tell, any control was not significant. Now, despite the offering of major productions from cultural centers of the world through our video services, smaller local production companies have remained useful and in demand enough that government support is still considered justified. It seems this approach is working well. The majority of even moderately qualified performers and venues, if sincerely dedicated to their craft, receive adequate financial compensation. Their remuneration does vary, of course, according to their proven capabilities, the size of their audiences, and the prominence of the locations where they perform.

Like today, a wide variety of sports were huge in the world of entertainment. All ages could participate at the amateur level in those days. Some people played in "sandlot" or "pickup" games, but much of the participation occurred in highly organized leagues, some sponsored by educational institutions, like today. Professional sports were very big businesses because of the number of people entertained by them. People would watch sports game in person as spectators and via live transmissions and recordings. Some of the sports that grew most popular were quite violent, both to participants in the organized competitions and even between fans of opposing teams. Live games took place in the stadiums of the times, and the broadcast media presented the games very thoroughly, often re-airing games and replaying particular plays or dramatic segments. All sports were also covered then by popular published paper media, such as "newspapers," magazines, and books. Even fan reactions, particularly ugly arguments and physical fights, were covered by the media of that day.

There were many other different forms of entertainment prevalent at the turn to the twenty-first century, and many performers and separately managed firms and organizations offered them up. Television was a separate media from "movies," which were projected on large screens in theater settings. There were also many "radio stations," which transmitted only sound. TV and sound stations were supported by advertisers, and clearly influenced listener desires for the promoted merchandise and services. Television offerings became very elaborate and diversified, originated by many independent networks and stations to satisfy a breadth of audience preferences, as well as to serve their advertisers. Movie theaters began serving up advertising as well. Most forms of recorded entertainment became another way of selling products to the public. For individuals to avoid advertising, they had to buy performances, even recorded ones, at higher prices.

Early in this century, a wide selection of movies and recorded sports began being offered on TV and through the "internet," like our media centers. Thus, began the integration of the media. Most of these separate entertainment outlets of course are long since gone, taken over by live and integrated transmission of musical and stage performances, world news broadcasting, and information-exchange programs across our present media spectrum. Occasionally there is the complaint that the news coverage we receive may be slanted because of government ownership. However, there is an agency (Truth in News, I believe) that is charged with ensuring presentations are honest, but the news is probably heavily influenced, if not controlled, by the Censoring for Health Agency.

In the past, there was also live and internet gaming. A city in Nevada became known as "Sin City" because it was open to all kinds of entertainment and behavior, profiting largely from gambling and other activity that is now illegal. For example, I believe in the late twentieth century Nevada was the only state of the union where prostitution was legal. Legal prostitution expanded to other areas before the government started the radical improvements leading to today's safe and peaceful environment for sexual activities.

Video gaming on our private monitors is of course even more popular today than it was a century ago, and I know you enjoy this. However, the time we can spend in such activities and the financial losses we can incur through them are carefully monitored and can be limited by the government when necessary. I think the government had difficulty catching gaming cheaters before the centralized locator/monitor systems were perfected and put into use.

Very prevalent then were individual and small groups of entertainers doing "floor shows" on small stages. Most were in the many alcoholic bars and restaurants. I am reminded of New Orleans, Louisiana, which still has the flavor of these times if not the full behavior. Besides musicians and singers, many floor shows included strippers, simulated sexual acts, and sometimes live sex performances. There were also "blue" sexually oriented movies available in special outlets and for use in private. This type of content moved fairly quickly into broadcast media. The subjects and content of books were not controlled in any way that I've found. Sexually explicit literature, "toys," and media were all widely available, although in some states stores that sold such things had to be out of range of schools. Unfortunately, there were many people, particularly men, who became addicted to sexual literature and media, then known as pornography, leading to serious family problems and much illicit behavior.

The advances in private communication devices back then allowed a lot of personal information exchange and private entertainment. But in some cases, private sexual "performances" also were captured on video or cell phone memories and transmitted to others. It was very hard to control who had access to such productions, and some serious embarrassments resulted. This sexually oriented material was also shown to be harmful to the youth, many of whom were largely the ones producing as well as watching it. It was also clearly proved that many individuals who were mentally challenged or handicapped responded to this more open atmosphere by using violent behavior for sexual satisfaction. Because of the influence of media, many more citizens accepted such action as normal.

Violence that was not related to sexual behavior, including the murder of innocents, was used by some to get noticed by the general public and the all-important media. Many such cases happened at schools and public meetings and even at military bases and entertainment centers. These incidents most often resulted in the death of the perpetrators but most times at the cost of others' lives and/or major injuries. There were cases where guns, knives, poisons, and even automobiles were the weapon of choice.

The quality and style of all forms of media varied quite widely, as did the costs and reimbursement mechanisms associated with providing it. But in general, most of it was available to the general population at affordable costs. In my view there were two main factors that caused most of the population, and their elected or otherwise powerful leaders at the time, to decide that very strong governmental intervention and control was required. As violence and perversion became a strong part of the plots and practices in entertainment, it also seemed to become more and more accepted, or at least expected, by the general population. The gradual acceptance or at least tolerance of such behavior grew rapidly into its practice, resulting in many injuries and deaths, often of uninvolved persons. Citizens lost property, health, and often their lives because there was little hesitation by some to use violence, often alcohol-or drug-induced, as part of thefts, simple altercations, and disagreements. Families lost children both physically and emotionally because of violence done to them. Many persons cycled in and out of prison because they continually perpetuated forms of violence on others. Kidnappers forced many young women and even young boys into prostitution. In some cases, these young people's parents or caregivers sold them into prostitution for economic reasons.

There were great costs to the general public to pay for crime-prevention attempts and to cover medical costs, damages to property, and the prison system. Education suffered from students' shift of interest to sex and violence and from the well-publicized acts of perversion by students as well as teachers on school grounds and campuses. The general public became more and more aware and sensitive to the personal threat to themselves and their families. Unfortunately, this awareness was often too late for many of the families. The damage that was done often lasted a lifetime. The general population also began to realize the significance of the related costs for control efforts passed through to them via taxation. When given the chance, they readily elected officials who promised to put a stop to the factors leading to such violence. As you know, eventually government officials did eliminate one proven negative influence that perpetuated such violence by taking active control of all media.

CHAPTER 5

EDUCATION

Andrew:

This topic ought to catch your interest. Although I have never heard that you might be planning a career in this direction, you are presently in the middle of your education. You may think my findings below more amusing than informative. It is hard to believe what bad shape the US education system was in at the turn of this century and how much things have improved since then. Your mother said you were having more difficulty than she expected at the university, but I know you will rise to the challenge.

The system of education in the US near the turn of the twenty-first century was in a pretty poor condition. Despite substantial publicity about poor testing results and a high dropout rate in public schools, the early remedial steps taken by federal and state programs and the local school districts were largely unsuccessful in overcoming poor academic results. Many placed blame on the lack of parental controls and the increase of violent behavior in public schools. Private schools were more successful but also so expensive that only a few could afford them. "Homeschooling," where parents or groups of parents directly administered their children's education, was legal and became much more popular. There certainly was a clear, noticeable difference in the grades and achievements of students whose parents were very active in their children's school life versus the growing number who just left it up to the students themselves and to the school system. When the administrative focus in public schools shifted to safety and improving the results of the students having the most difficulty, overall results in public education waned.

The burden of the large expense increases in the academic area was further amplified by the increased need to support public school programs such as feeding students. Meal programs had been set up to ensure that the children of poorer families had proper nutrition. Even appropriate uniforms and clothes were often supplied to the less fortunate at a cost to the general public. Many argued that educating noncitizens brought into the US by their alien parents was inappropriate and expensive and encouraged illegal immigration. It very clearly added much to the financial burden of education. Higher direct taxing by school systems and increased federal spending did not seem to have the desired effects. Then, during the major economic downturn on both sides of the year 2010, funds for public education began to be reduced, further hindering educational results as well as increasing the dropout rate.

Despite the apparent lack of success in public education systems, higher education attendance increased during this period. More and more young people were going to college, and many of them financed their education with federal-guaranteed loans with liberal terms. During the long 2007–2014 recession, or downturn, more and more jobless young people attended colleges. They predominately used the federally backed and readily accessible student loan programs to cover their tuition and related expenses. The national balance that was owed on these loans reached unexpectedly high levels because of this increased utilization. The debt burden on newly graduated students prevented them from initially living the lifestyles they had expected and kept many from being able to start families. During the extended recession of that time period, many newer graduates could not find appropriate employment, and there was a high level of student loan default and a substantial threat of even more. Severe cutbacks in the student loan program and increased pressure for repayment was considered unhealthy, potentially causing a further depressing impact on the US economy.

Private educational establishments at the prep school, collegiate, and postgraduate levels seemed better able to produce good academic results. These educational institutions grew substantially during the last half of the twentieth century. However, the ever-higher tuition required because of the increasing expenses for operating the smaller institutions severely limited admissions. This problem became more prevalent as economic conditions worsened and taxes on Middle America increased. Some education researchers also argued that the children of the families that could afford private education did not fully take advantage of the higher-quality experience their parents' money bought. These researchers felt the better education that these students received was at least partially wasted, since these richer young people often did not choose careers that benefited the general public welfare.

The financial demands on the public higher education systems added significantly and directly to private debt and to the US national debt. This was due to both the increased spending required in publicly supported schools and the fact that many of the student loans for college-aged students went unpaid and had to be written off—that is, absorbed by the taxpayers. The impact also showed up in other ways. Young people without work opportunities could and evidentially did yield substantial unrest and subsequent trouble. These folks needed an alternative such as further education to consume their time until the economy could provide jobs for them. The government had no real choice but to continue the risky student loan programs.

Educators agreed on many known problems hampering the effectiveness of the educational system. There were suitable answers to fix these problems and at a reasonably predictable cost. However, the solutions only began to be forthcoming quite a few years later after effective funding mechanisms were agreed upon and implemented.

The situation is so different today. Appropriate education for all is basically free, with the government covering tuition and all other expenses, except housing and living costs. Students of course must qualify for the level and kind of higher education they will receive. The extensive testing and continual qualification exams keep the system both fair and efficient. National workforce needs are also considered in the process of matching students to the optimum type of education and training. Psychological testing and counseling are part of this process, leading generally to complete individual and family satisfaction with the plan developed for each student.

You, my great-grandson, should be a fine example of the success of the system. Don't you agree?

CHAPTER 6

ENVIRONMENT AND SAFETY

Andrew:

Another area of critical change during the period we are studying was concern about the environment. Big strides were made over a twenty-year period—a long time—but there was considerable resistance because of the costs involved, disagreement over the needs, and the absolute requirement for worldwide cooperation to be successful. When the critical problems were publicized and the scientific community overwhelmingly and publically agreed to them, things finally moved along. Still, multinational cross-financing had to be made available to produce results.

The United States made great strides in the late twentieth century in improving the air, water, and land quality that had become a growing health hazard accompanying industrialization and population growth. Similarly, manufactured goods and foodstuffs standards were carefully examined and found in need of control. Quality standards were reevaluated, found wanting, and gradually tightened up as scientific evidence mounted about dangers of inaction. Pollution from the automobiles and trucks of the day was legislated down over a period of years that allowed automakers time to alter their product designs. Tobacco legislation was another powerful example at the consumer level. For many years the smoking of tobacco had been growing among the populations of the world. In the US, as negative health aspects of smoking became clear, strong legislation and prosecution of companies that had knowingly caused citizens to become addicted combined with required media warnings and substantially higher taxes on tobacco products reduced the population of tobacco users in the US by over 70 percent.

Addressing international environmental concerns, including tobacco use, was more difficult. Countries independently made decisions about tobacco and other potentially harmful products, as well as individual plant emission limits. However, global warming and atmospheric pollution became huge worldwide issues. Air quality had been studied and debated for many years. For the first half of the twentieth century in the US there was only minimal agreement and little pollutant-reduction progress. A governmental agency, the Environmental Protection Agency (EPA), was formed to develop scientifically sound testing and appropriate restrictions for business and industry emission levels at the plant or facility level. The laws had to be thorough and consistent for all polluters. The EPA's effort to determine acceptable levels of effluents and abatement requirements between plants and companies was effective although also very controversial and costly. Implementation of the new standards was slow, and these expenses had to be passed on to the consumer through higher prices.

Similarly, there was little agreement among worldwide industrialists and shippers about the degradation of the oceans and large international waters, both as to seawater quality and waste accumulation, and there was no real action to address these issues. Overfishing was another measurable problem where lack of appropriate and effective legal precedent plus plain old greed led to little control over the worldwide fishing industry. Other overharvesting was clearly observed, such as with trees in the Amazon basin and wildlife in parts of southern Africa. The requirement for international cooperation was fruitless until much later when it was clearly shown that the whole world was on an environmentally devastating downhill slope.

Historical practices of US industries had left many dangerous blemishes, including abandoned facilities and industrial dump sites. Government officials agreed to force the parties that had created these blemishes to clean them up. However, lack of knowledge of who these parties were and the extent of the customers' divided responsibility made this chore very tough. Often, the actual owners of the dump sites had long since abandoned their now-illegal locations. The records covering the extent that companies had participated in dumping their waste materials were also scant. The problems of identification of responsible parties and the small government budgets for detection and remediation resulted in minimal cleanup of these potentially dangerous waste-material repositories. Some of these are still problems today.

Unsafe industrial structures, equipment, and practices were also prevalent. Many companies, although certainly not all, often put short-term profit ahead of the welfare of their employees, contract workers, and surrounding communities. Although technology, procedures, and equipment were available to enhance safety in the workplace, practices were very uneven in the US until the federal government got involved. A series of refinery explosions, offshore tanker spills, and petroleum platform accidents helped stimulate serious environmental concerns. A continuously tougher set of standards was developed, measurement systems were put into place, and a new organization, the National Safety Administration, began to enforce safe practices. Research continues today on methods and equipment to prevent harmful accidents and to outlaw risky operating practices in situations that can, and still do, turn carelessness and equipment failures into dangers harmful to individuals, towns, and the environment.

A big hindrance to continuing environmental improvement is balancing the benefits with the high cost of pollution detection and abatement as well as the interference in personal choice that tougher standards impose. I guess this will be a continuing debate that will engender more and more research and field investigations and therefore interesting career opportunities.

Considering this major, Andrew?

CHAPTER 7

MEDICINE

Andrew:

It is truly an amazing exercise for me to look back and consider the state of medicine and health and related issues of those earlier times versus today. I guess, in my younger years, health was not much of a problem for me. As I thought on it some, I did recall complicated health problems the older members of our family and their friends fought, some to the death. Even younger people suffered. I can remember some of my classmates having health-related absences, and a couple of my college friends even dropped out due to illnesses. The subsequent health-care improvements that took place in our country and the world are just amazing. We are so lucky now to receive the substantial benefits from both the enhancement of our nation's health and the reduction of resources required to maintain a healthy population.

I was very surprised to hear from your mother that you have had some recent minor issues with your health. You take care of yourself. Don't forget that I need your help to carry out this project.

There was a long period in the twentieth century when the physical and mental health of our nation appeared to decline substantially, although life span was going up. Part of this apparent decline may have just been the positive progress in detecting illnesses and diseases that were already prevalent but simply had not been identified. Some accused companies in the health industry of overpromoting their remedies for major and minor ailments. However, medical developments did have a rapidly and continuously expanding horizon. Life expectancy rose over 15 percent from midcentury to 2000. But the costs of treatment and hospitalization skyrocketed. Health insurance was almost universally a required employment benefit. Although existence of such programs was pretty standard, the specific programs themselves were very uneven. Individual employers made different choices on their benefit programs, and the workers, who paid part of their salaries for these benefits, also had a variety of options, including not taking the insurance.

The federal government was also heavily involved in helping to cover some of the health-care costs for retired, handicapped, and unemployed or underemployed citizens. Military veterans' care was considered a government obligation, though quality varied between locations. The result was that across the populace there was very uneven health service, substantially dependent on an individual's ability to pay and their employer's choices on insurance coverage. The costs supported by the government got higher and higher, but still a substantial percentage of the population, such as illegal aliens and the extremely poor, were not covered or were under-covered. Some doctors and hospitals insisted they could not afford to accept patients who could not pay, so they had to restrict intake and turned many away. Emergency room service demands at major hospitals grew rapidly because the medical code of ethics of that time did not allow them to refuse emergency patients. Many hospitals closed their emergency rooms as a result.

The president elected in 2008 promised a new national program enhancing "Medicare" to solve coverage unevenness and to include all citizens in health-care coverage. The legislation became active despite substantial disagreement but was later delayed and revised dramatically due to the higher-than-expected costs and the projections of future expenditures in a period when the government was in severe financial stress.

There were many other major medical system problems and pressures during this period, including the increase of the average age accompanied by the substantial improvements in late-life health care. At that time, about 85 percent of a person's health expenses occurred in the last ten years of life, which made up about 12.5 percent of their life expectancy at that time. There was also clear national-scale health damage caused by air and water pollution, the use of tobacco products and illegal drugs, and a vast overuse of legal medications. Injuries, particularly from automotive accidents and crimes, were also a big factor in increasing health-care demands. Although major strides were being made in the detection and treatment of prevalent illnesses, such as cancer, these strides were not without accompanying major increases in costs to cover research as well as the treatments themselves. To control expenditures, the government insurance programs had very specific upper limits on payments for treatment of all illnesses and injuries. Some of the best doctors began to refuse to accept patients on government insurance because of these limits.

Unfortunately, there was also a lot of cheating in this system, consisting largely of insurance fraud. Companies and some individual doctors collected insurance payments for services they did not really perform. Some doctors and medical units ordered medical tests and treatments that were not really needed. Sometimes this was done in collusion with "patients," who shared in the illicit payments. Government and private insurance accounting systems were so complicated that payments to individuals and medical facilities were sometimes made although no actual services were rendered. Automobile accidents were faked or intentionally caused to allow collection of insurance benefits. These extra costs were never well quantified but were believed to be very significant.

The easy availability and widespread overuse of prescription drugs, often illegally obtained, created another kind of problem. People used these drugs, usually painkillers and anxiety medications, to induce artificial, short-term highs or lows. When some very prominent entertainment stars died of overdoses of medication formulated to be used only in serious medial situations, such as for surgical anesthesiology, many investigations followed, and some doctors involved in such overdosing were tried, convicted and imprisoned. Although there were many other similar cases of drug-related deaths in the entertainment world, they rarely resulted in legal action. As these cases hit the news, it also became obvious that the general public was just as involved in the overuse of prescription drugs. This overuse was detectable by comparing the known quantity of drugs manufactured and sold versus the estimated actual medical requirements. Drug companies, many doctors, and their patients all derived benefits from these practices, although the patient "benefits" were only for the short term and often actually proved very costly to them in the longer run, including many deaths.

Another facet of these phenomena was the broader allowance of legal sale of some previously illegal products, such as marijuana. Marijuana legalization in many states effectively institutionalized the recreational use of a formerly illegal substance. This decision benefitted marijuana farmers, prescribing doctors, and specialized pharmacies, but the costs to society and eventually to the government were substantial, adding to the many other problems of the time.

What a difference from today! Accidental and inflicted injuries in the United States have been substantially reduced by the control of criminal activity, the many transportation safety improvements, and the elimination or better design of many potentially harmful or dangerous products. Now most major disease categories have been eliminated, or prevention methods and successful, quick cures have been found. Everybody in the US, and to some degree in most of the world, is healthy essentially all his or her life. The whole world has benefitted from the elimination of or control of disease-causing substances, including germs and pollutants. These improvements, combined with the amazing progress of our national medical programs, effectively give everybody in the US a full lifetime of good health. The full miracle for us comes from starting good health practices early, including adjusting genetic attributes at the preconception level, and from implementing a wide range of appropriate preventative practices, including the adjustment of bodily fluids and the transplanting of critical organs when needed.

Our present lifetime program of tailored medications is also critical to our good health. I understand that most of our daily pills are standard, but some are unique to the individual, offsetting or allowing for age, unadjusted genetic differences, and health history. The physical measurements taken in our daily online therapy sessions detect potential health problems as well as determine that the right pills have been taken. Now our local Monitor MPs quickly follow up on any deviations or required changes, and they can require immediate counseling sessions if people do not seem cooperative.

Medical costs for health are now considerably lower than at the turn to this century. Early and continuing maintenance and preventative measures far more than offset the previous costs of healing via curative medications, procedures, and practices. Even medical research expenditures now are far lower, although efforts continue as the health-giving profession seeks even further improvements.

To me the downside is the over-one-hundred thing that I now face. Somewhere it was decided that life maintenance beyond one hundred years—a little arbitrary, I believe—is not justified. This is where the farms take charge. In a few years I will move to my assigned one, and my maintenance medications will be dropped. I guess individuals age pretty quickly without them, and historic life expectations rule. The farms are supposedly fun places to be, with great living conditions, excellent recreation opportunities, and lots of special entertainment, which can go beyond the normal rules. Great new friendships, though short-lived, can develop or old ones be continued, if you can maneuver to the same place as present same-age friends.

I know that there are also some younger people at the farms, although I am not sure how well they fit in. As you know, if an individual runs out of money—that is, if their financial balance actually goes to zero—they also are sent to a farm. Most folks avoid this through loans from friends and relatives, but not all can. In addition, younger workers are needed at the farms. I understand it is a job for some but a prison sentence for others. I know people of your age don't think about, much less anticipate, running out of money. As you get older, you will need to carefully balance your spending versus income to ensure you don't fit into this category of farmers.

I guess this is all really OK by me. I have had a full, productive, and fun life, and to a degree I am looking forward to my time at the farm and to eventually meeting my maker, as well as Evelyn and other departed loved ones, in the hereafter in which I, and many others, sincerely believe.

CHAPTER 8

FAMILIES

Andrew:

Couples composed of one man and one woman, with or without children, are still, although barely, the most prevalent families, but there is a very wide variety of other groupings as well. Today other family units are legally defined, approved, and monitored. Family units can consist of any number of members of any age and any sexual orientation. All family formations and any changes to family units must be reported for approval. Family units are continuously monitored, particularly to ensure they are performing properly to create a healthy environment for underage children. In cases where appropriate goals are not being reached, children are moved to a different, carefully chosen family.

In family units there are no or very few differences between individual members' privileges, and these differences must be specifically defined by reason, such as age or mental capacities. There can of course also be temporary exceptions to privileges, like for injuries or pregnancies.

It is very interesting how the concept and definition of family has changed. In the twentieth century it seems family meant a married man and woman plus their offspring and sometimes one or both sets of the couple's living parents. In some ethnic or economic circumstances, family groups included brothers, sisters, and other relatives of the couple all living together. For a family then, the central couple was legally married, and in most cases, any other family members were blood relatives of one of them.

Many of the laws of the land at that time only recognized marriage and strict family ties as the legal standard.

By the start of the twenty-first century, the previous concept of family had changed dramatically for several reasons. Many government incentives, including higher benefit payments to unmarried mothers, encouraged divorces, if not necessarily real separations. In divorce court proceedings, "irreconcilable differences" was often the legal justification given. Many times, there were major legal arguments over dividing joint estates. Divorce was popularly headlined by prominent show business personalities, including professional sports figures, whose marriages were often short-lived. Over 50 percent of all marriages ended in divorce for one reason or another, leaving the individuals the opportunity to marry again, possibly multiple times. Adultery—marriage partners becoming sexually involved outside of the marriage—was often a cause for separation and divorce. Physical abuse and even murder of family members, including children, was not that unusual and in many cases was well documented in the press. Marriage was often delayed, but successful first marriages with original families still became rarer and rarer.

It also became more acceptable for family groups to exist outside the husband-wife boundaries. Because of the high divorce rate among married couples, there were many single-parent families, possibly with other relatives living with the single parent. In addition, unmarried couples often lived together, for both the sexual and economic advantages, and often with one or both pair's children included. This was not illegal, although many considered it unhealthy or immoral. "Gays" or homosexuals and others earlier considered sexual deviants were sometimes allowed to be legally partnered as a couple. Some states, after much debate, legalized such gay marriages. Gradually political pressure at the national level built from these individuals and their organizations to liberalize both marriage and the governmentally derived benefits of marriage. Many states began to legalize same-sex marriages and altered related state-controlled factors such as property ownership, taxes, and benefit payments. During these times a major shift in federal law occurred, as did the governmental role in family matters in the redefinition of family.

As you know, sexual activities are now entirely separate from childbearing activities with the latter carefully controlled by appropriate governmental bodies. Couples or families wishing to procreate must apply for and receive approval and the proper medications to have children. This family system was promulgated to accomplish a number of goals, including population control, security of individuals, and the limitation of unwanted children. "Happier" families and more successful family life resulted. National population control today considers the total number of people in a certain area and in the US as a whole as well as the broader economic situation. Population control is also aimed at preventing children being born or raised in improper financial circumstances or in situations considered unhealthy for them from a psychological point of view. Children are quickly moved between families when an unhealthy situation is detected. This is done with very careful mental counseling for the children and both families to ensure success.

Today, of course, a family group may have a broad range of participants, but it is very rigorously documented and controlled. Our families now can be based on traditional man-woman couples and blood relatives or can include any willing citizens who agree to be defined as such. Although these defined families must be carefully documented and approved as such by the government, the group can be changed and on relatively short notice. The family makeup is fluid but must be formally legalized anytime there is a change. All through this century, our own family has chosen to remain as blood relatives much as in the previous century, but our approach is becoming the exception, not the rule.

Since present governmental financial and information systems are oriented strictly to the individual, it is not a difficult matter to regroup families as soon as a new makeup is approved. There are many government records, including those related to taxation and benefit plans, that must be shifted or combined differently, but these are also quickly accommodated. The government-employed MPs for a family are instantly aware of the approved changes. In fact, most of them already know that changes are forthcoming because of their daily monitoring sessions and their instantaneous and continuous knowledge of an individual's activities and movements. The MPs are often directly involved and are certainly aware of needs that require counseling prior to a family redefinition. Usually if some family member is becoming out of place or appears dissatisfied with their family situation, the MPs are the first to be aware of the problem and can take action quickly.

I believe the benefits of the present controls are obvious. The system prevents serious disagreements or other kinds of upsets within a family. In the past such issues were often a source of family mental trauma, abuse, or even murder. Unsuccessful marriages, which were a major source of unhappiness and even physical abuse, no longer require lengthy and expensive settlement. A marriage's lack of success is also hard to hide. In the case of ownership and estate values, each family member's individual wealth and entitlements are defined continuously and are totally portable. If a family's makeup changes, so does the family's financial situation but not the individual's. I also believe that the daily attitude pills and monitoring of mental condition assist in family stability, so that previously prevalent individual dissatisfaction and dangerous family situations are much less frequent.

CHAPTER 9

RELIGION

Andrew:

In the last one hundred years religious practices in the US have changed at least as dramatically as our studies have discovered that everything else has. An overview would say religion has moved from a very large, public practice to a very small, personal one.

In the twentieth century in the US, religion meant "church." Believers would gather in a public building, or church, for almost all their religious activities. Every city, even small towns, would have multiple church buildings depending on denominational preferences and the popularity of the church leaders. This was of course not dissimilar to practices that had been found around the world for centuries. Although the basic beliefs, practices, and approach to leadership varied, places of worship were common for all recorded time. However, it is apparent from history that religion was often used as a way to maintain an existing ruling hierarchy. Leaders often took advantage of past populaces, which like today had an inborn desire to believe in a greater power, through the unscrupulous use of religion and religious practices. The history of religion is a very interesting topic, and I must almost force myself to concentrate on only the most recent changes.

The public practice of the traditional religions has been substantially reduced in the last 150 years. Around the middle of the twentieth century, church membership and attendance was a part of most lives. US religious practice centered mostly on Christian denominations, with probably over

90 percent of people identifying as Christian. The acceptance of other religions, such as Islam and Eastern religions, was very low, and even Judaism operated largely in the shadows except for large cities. Prior to the 1950s, in many of the southern and western states, even Catholics kept a low profile. It was 1960, for example, before the first Catholic US president was elected. His opposition raised the political issue of whether he would take some of his orders from the pope in Italy. Freedom of religion as guaranteed in the US Constitution was upheld, but the social structures then in place did not guarantee acceptance.

Gradually, however, along with a shift away from previous church denominations, the prejudice between religions faded considerably. By 2010, alongside Christian churches, there were many mosques for Muslims; temples and shrines for Buddhists, Shintoists, Hindus, and Sikhs; and other religious houses of worship in large and medium-sized American cities. During this time, atheists also became more public and vocal. In fact they were successful in getting many Christian and other public religious practices, such as prayers at community events and public schools, outlawed. They were also successful at forcing stricter interpretation of the constitutionally required separation of religion and state, arguing that government buildings and monuments could not display religious symbols or quotations. Closer to the present there was a large public debate before a Supreme Court decision forced removal of the previous national motto—In God We Trust—from US currency.

Some of the changes were made more generally acceptable because of some truly weird practices and events that the press enthusiastically covered. For example, members of certain religious groups sold their worldly possessions because their leaders convinced them that God had communicated an end of the world on such and such a date. In the South, several hugely popular religious leaders were exposed and ousted because they used contributions to their causes to enrich themselves. Some popular religious leaders were brought down after exposure of sexual affairs and practices, again widely publicized. In the 1970s in Jonestown, Guyana, over nine hundred people from a religious community of Americans committed suicide at their leader's instruction after he was threatened with legal investigations because of his financial reporting. This Jonestown event in South America included many parents killing their own children.

The demise of religion was also furthered by religious scandals. Around the world, beginning in the early 2000s, the Catholic Church suffered great setbacks from the publicity of cases of priests sexually abusing children. Catholic organizations from parishes all the way to the Vatican were sued, predominantly by men who as children had been sexually abused by priests. These priests, like all their peers, had sworn sexual abstinence to enter the priesthood. The Catholic Church had little choice but to settle thousands of claims, mostly out of court and often for large sums of money. Although there were publicized cases in the US of dishonest ministers bilking their congregations and media followers out of thousands and even millions of dollars, nothing approached the publicity or the cost of the Catholic sexual abuse cases.

Around the turn of the century there were more controversies that added to the slow demise of religion. Two issues that became larger and more critical were the eligibility of gays to pastor Christian churches and the acceptable definition of marriage itself. The more general rights of gays in society were also being redefined. In the eyes of the law as well as organized religion, marriage was traditionally considered to be between a man and a woman. Committed gay couples successfully fought legal battles in all states to be recognized as legal partners for tax and employment benefits and other financial matters. However, the debate over the acceptance of these partnerships as "marriages" continued, both legally and within the religious denominations. This debate was particularly difficult in Christian churches, where their Holy Bible seemed to be very clear on the definition of marriage and the sin of homosexuality. Many churches and some major religious denominations split over these issues, and many, many individuals, not just gays, became disenchanted with religion in general.

Another of the monotheistic religions, Islam, had a similar moral orientation as Christianity. However, during this same time, many terroristic acts in the US against its citizens as well as in other countries clearly stemmed from Muslims. Certainly not all followers of Islam believed it was their duty to either convert or kill all non-Muslims, but some seemed to believe thusly. In many cases such Islamists probably used religion as an excuse for organizing profitable and, in many cases, illegal activities, such as extortion, smuggling, and kidnapping. They also received funds from

Muslim organizations, particularly in oil-rich countries, possibly without the givers' understanding of how the contributions were to be used. The Taliban in Afghanistan once used their particular strict belief system as both justification for and as a model for governing a country.

Many destructive events were attempted in the name of the Muslim religion. Many of these events were successful in killing Americans, as well as Europeans and other citizens of the world. Many terrorist acts were centered on public transportation systems, including commercial airlines. The US government took dramatic and costly steps in an attempt to safeguard against such acts and to find and punish guilty parties. An example was the airport terminal reconfigurations and changes to check-in procedures for the flying public and their baggage to minimize the opportunity for in-flight threats to be successful. Designated agents flew disguised as ordinary passengers on many flights. Some of the cost increase was borne by the flying public, but most was accounted for by taxation to cover the direct, continuing government expenditures. Less publicized but also quite expensive were the many changes required to add safeguards to protect industrial, utility, and communication systems.

Excepting the related terrorism-protection costs, the broadening of religious practices and the reduction in practicing believers had little effect on US economic success, although the issues consumed an inordinate amount of time for state and federal legislators and courts. However, the decline of religion in general was quite possibly one of the causes of the change in the national behavior. The decline of honesty, fairness, and mutual helpfulness undoubtedly did contribute to increases in crime as well as decreases in family values and the previous inclination toward neighbor-to-neighbor assistance versus government help. These changes very obviously did raise governmental and private citizen costs.

As you know from our own family practices through the years, we have tried to maintain our Christian principles and practices from the old days. Though there are many Americans doing likewise, this is certainly not the general case in the US anymore. Formal Christian practices, along with those of other religions, have become substantially less prevalent as well as more transparent. Still, there are many positives for the general public from having active and generous believers and practitioners. Perhaps some governmental cost reduction has even been realized from the national system of citizen observation, tracking, and control. It is clear that being dishonest or hurtful to others is a lot less possible today because of effective observation and enforcement, rather than through religious belief systems. However, the current national monitoring system is certainly quite expensive.

CHAPTER 10

ILLEGAL DRUGS

Andrew:

You probably know something here that I don't, since I believe it was people not far from your age that in the middle of the twentieth century popularized the use of illegal drugs—mostly hallucinatory drugs and painkillers, I think. With the daily testing that goes on now, I doubt whether anything like illicit drug use exists today. I am under the understanding that part of our present daily-pills routine solves the problem of us feeling the need for or wanting anything like formerly illegal drugs. The required daily therapy sessions at everyone's home info center also would reveal the use of any illegal medication or any signs of unhappiness to our MPs, so that psychotherapy or medical treatment sessions could quickly be scheduled to fix such problems

I would certainly appreciate your frank observations on this subject if you think I missed anything important.

Hallucinatory and pain-killing substances have been around a long time, originating in the Far East, I believe, but legally moving to Western societies hundreds of years ago. It was a long time before the danger and damage of using these were recognized and their use was made illegal in most of the world. Organized crime quickly recognized the profit potential of illegal substances that were habit forming. Most all regular drug users were "hooked," as I think they used to say, meaning if they couldn't get their drugs, they suffered severe pain in withdrawal. After some amount of use, they were addicted and had no comfortable physical choice except to continue consuming these illegal substances. If they did not have the money needed to support their habit, they were willing to steal, prostitute themselves, or even kill for it—and they did so. Adding to this direct damage, the business of supplying illegal drugs became a major criminal activity, causing an ever-larger requirement for police, prisons, and legal resources. I plan to review the documents on the whole legal process itself later.

The illegal drug supply system became more and more sophisticated, with new habit-forming substances introduced almost faster than they could be declared illegal. It seemed the young adult population and some minority groups originally led the way into drug use in the US. In the early years of drug popularization, many people your age dropped out of college and early careers to join groups or communes dedicated to drug use. Sexual attitudes also became a lot looser in these settings. I don't know the real connection here, but sex liberalization and drug use both seemed to start about the same time, in the 1960s or so, coincident with a very unpopular US war in Southeast Asia. As many of these young people grew up, they continued drug use. Drugs were also indirectly promoted by people in the entertainment world, who were copied in many other ways as well, although they were hardly good role models for young people. In fact, in the show business population there were many highly publicized drug-induced missteps and many "accidental" deaths from overdoses.

Illegal drugs grew very fast and very big. In the early 2010s the drug trade was then estimated to be worth over $500 billion in the US, with most of the drugs purified or manufactured elsewhere and illegally imported into this country. Later the drug problem became even more widespread and sophisticated as legal drugs developed for killing pain and combating depression were marketed to people who did not need them medically. There were many licensed physicians whose chief business was selling prescriptions for these drugs. Attempts to control this form of drug activity were costly and largely ineffective. Some states also began legalizing certain of the formerly illegal drugs.

So drugs and related activity grew into a large problem on many counts. Drugs had a huge direct impact on the home life of citizens and their work performance in business and government, as well as on individuals' actions to acquire the money to buy them. The costs for law enforcement and incarceration increased commensurately, as did the costs for the legal system to process these crimes. Government efforts to stop illegal international drug trafficking were very expensive and largely ineffective. Increased competition between the criminals in the drug trade caused a lot of periphery violence, frequently injuring innocent bystanders. The trade also corrupted many officials and law enforcement personnel, who were paid by people in the drug supply and sales business to clear the way for their very profitable criminal activity.

Common folk's concerns grew on several fronts. First was the threat of potential drug dependence to their children, relatives, and friends, as well as the potential violence that needy users and warring drug gangs might inflict on their families. They were also keenly aware of the taxes they were paying for largely ineffective protection and government attempts to diminish this trade. Drugs became another front where citizen safety diminished while the cost of trying to ensure that safety hit pocketbooks directly as well as pushing local, state, and federal taxes ever higher.

CHAPTER 11

VIOLENT CRIME

Andrew:

It appears to me, dear great-grandson, that one of the primary reasons why Americans wanted or were willing to make the substantial lifestyle changes to our new era was violent crime. Many, many people were affected directly, and those that were not were frightened that the well-publicized crimes could happen to them or their loved ones. They also realized that they were financially paying for all this crime in many ways. You have certainly never seen and probably never even heard about some of the examples I will give you in this communiqué. But I am certain that after review, you will agree that change was badly needed. Whether there were other solutions that would have worked better I don't know. Many were tried but were hugely expensive and mostly ineffective. Fortunately, the dramatic measures the government eventually took seem to have worked.

VIOLENT CRIME

It is somewhat surprising to us today how violent crimes were so much a problem around the turn of the century. Even family disagreements often led to violence, some of it surprisingly harmful and even deadly. Some parents abused their own children. The breadth and extent of criminal activity such as robbery and rape meant that most everyone lived in fear. Many carried firearms for protection (it was legal then). Willingness and tendency to use these guns increased with the preponderance of them. Accidents with such firearms that caused unintended harm were also common. Mentally incompetent, severely emotionally upset, and some impossible-to-understand Americans who relished personal publicity carried out surprisingly unpredictable rampages using firearms. Individuals sometimes perpetrated such violent criminal acts because they wanted revenge for some past insult or occurrence, such as being fired from their job. Violent, terroristic acts were also harmful to many, but these will be covered in my separate notes on terrorism.

Easy gun availability promoted armed robberies that often ended with the firing of those guns. Most often the violators used weapons to acquire material things symbolic of a lifestyle that they could not afford with the job talents and work ethic they possessed. Citizens also often used armed robbery to support what was then called a "drug habit." As discussed separately, drug use itself often left people out of control so that they would commit acts far outside their normal behavior, and very clearly the industry that provided the illegal drugs was violence ridden.

Law enforcement itself became increasingly violent, partly because of the preponderance of weapons available to those involved in criminal acts. Use of deadly weapons by both sides of the law grew with their easy availability and increased sophistication. Police brutality and accidental shootings grew with the risks the officers sensed they were taking. However, the legal process for the criminals arrested was slow and very lenient compared to today. Then, many detained law abusers were paroled or released almost as soon as they were arrested, partly due to the cost of incarceration. For those found guilty, prison sentences could be different between states and even between judges, who operated very independently. Prisons were many, and they were often overpopulated and were not often corrective. They even seemed to reinforce criminal behavior, leading to even more criminal activity after prisoners completed their sentences. In our predecessor's files, I read that over 2 percent of those living in the US resided in prisons in 2000. Maintaining the prison system was expensive, and sometimes sentences were shortened so the cities and states could save money. The need for prison space even led cash-strapped authorities to begin utilizing privately owned prisons, run as businesses by nongovernmental groups.

Robberies occurred everywhere and anytime. Street corners and parking lots (needed for personal cars in those days) were often the scenes of crimes. Homes were burglarized, sometimes even with the folks living there present, and often this was not good for their health! Robbers would often pick up postal packages and even outdoor furniture from victims' front doors. Businesses were frequently robbed. What they called "convenience stores" in those days were frequent targets, because they were small, located everywhere, and had little security in place. When owners and operators armed themselves, shootings increased. Armed criminals robbed other stores, particularly those with valuable merchandise, as well as many banks during business hours as well as after closing time in "break-ins." There were many commercial and retail banks located in accessible public buildings in those days. These banks still carried currency, such as we still see in some other countries. Such robberies often resulted in physical harm and sometimes the death of innocent people. There were also "kidnappings," where criminals would capture and hold victims for ransom or, worse, as slaves, forcing them into prostitution or using them for their own sexual pleasure. Governmental entities threw money at these problems through more law enforcement officers, stricter penalties, and more prisons, but that did not seem to improve things significantly.

I believe that what substantially eliminated the crime problem was both the large improvement in financial well-being for all today and the use of additional and advanced detection methods, combined with quick punitive incarceration. The implanted tracking devices everyone carries now and the electronic detection systems that are omnipresent ensure that the authorities know where anyone is, or has been, at any time. So if there is criminal activity, there is very little chance of it going undetected or of the individuals not being arrested. There is not much publicity about this, maybe because there are so few cases and there's instantaneous assessment, but I know that today persons with violent or criminal tendencies are sent to specialized rehabilitation camps. It is rumored that if a person cannot be cured, he or she doesn't come back but is permanently removed from society, unlike the old prison system.

Presently our medications and our automated psychotherapy devices seem to reduce the tendency to want or think we need more than we have, or at least they eliminate our willingness to take things from others by illegal or forceful means. Of course it is now a crime not to take our standard medications or to pass up the daily time with the psychotherapy system connected to our home communication centers. The system quickly detects if we skip either our meds or the health-and-counseling session, and enforcement action is also quick. I admit I have forgotten the pills more than once, but our neighborhood MP arrived in my home quickly to see that I corrected my error. Of course, such forgetfulness or related errors showed up immediately on my financial statement, which means I paid my penalty and therefore had to give up something else that I wanted.

What the government had to do to develop and pay for all these prevention and detection capabilities is another story that I plan on digging into later.

CHAPTER 12

WHITE-COLLAR CRIME

Dear Andrew,

This section is related to my research and comments on crime and drugs but covers a different problem—criminal activity where bodily harm was very unusual but that, besides being costly to business, put demands on the justice system and therefore US government expenditures. In some cases the crimes were motivated by drug use and could evolve into violence, but the crimes addressed here have to do with business and financial transactions. The "white-collar" moniker came about because of the fact that most of the culprits did this criminal activity while on their jobs, and in the old days office workers, or at least men, wore white collared shirts to their work.

There was a very broad spectrum of such criminal activity by 2010, and it had become very damaging to the pocketbooks of many US citizens. I would say there was probably only a very small portion of the population that was *not* somehow taken advantage of economically by this side of criminality. Shoplifting and pickpocketing were simple examples. Stealing goods from an employer was another. Bookkeeping and accounting robberies, called embezzlements, mounted. Cheating on government subsidies and benefits was rampant. For the years after World War II it appears all kinds of white-collar robbery became more and more expansive as well as creative.

There were some spectacular larger schemes. In particular, the headlines of that day included details and followed the legal due process of many

"Ponzi scheme" manipulators who were caught. Some of these schemes led to total investor losses in the billions of dollars, a lot of money today but even more then. These sophisticated crooks would take advantage of others by promising participants unusually high returns on their personal investments in a business or investment scheme. They would many times deliver on their promises of exorbitant returns or dividends but would do so not from the earnings on the investments but from the new principal that was being increasingly entrusted to them. They used a portion of the incoming funds as they pleased, including for their own benefit in high living or hidden bank accounts.

All these schemes required an increasing flow of investor money to work. At some point, usually when new money stopped coming in or was not enough to cover promised returns, the scheme failed. Then the perpetrators usually disappeared with the money. In some cases, tax agents and government investigators discovered and revealed the schemes. However, in most of such cases they either didn't figure it out, or after they discovered it, they greedily became included as part of the scheme. Although the corporate names of such schemes usually included the term *investment*, eventually the investments the perpetrators did make did not cover the exorbitant dividends they were paying their clients and the monies they were using for their own benefit. Then they were forced to take such bold steps that their schemes were more easily exposed.

There were many other forms of these Ponzi schemes. For example, I found our ancestor had examples of solicitations for money that provided little except the promise that if you sent your money in for x (where x could be a book, course, or inspirational video, for example) and convinced ten or more others to do the same, you could expect to get back a healthy sum in return by earning some portion of the sales made by the others you brought in and those that they and further "downstream" participants brought in. The solicitors would deliver your book and then payments of part of the cash they received from those you were responsible for bringing in. When the number of new participants dwindled, the solicitors would often disappear with the profits, using them to satisfy their own desires.

Other schemes were less complicated but just as insidious. Many smart accountants of the day learned to "cook the books," and this occurred at many levels. Small company and nonprofit accountants turned embezzlers were at the less sophisticated end. For example, in paying bills, an embezzler would often forge invoices from a false entity or one that they individually controlled and make payments to it from their employer's bank account. This was hard to detect in small businesses with few employees. Individuals in larger corporations used much more sophisticated accounting trickery, involving much-larger amounts of money. Many times, several employees had to collude to make these schemes work.

The sums were usually much larger when such accounting trickery was used by the corporations themselves. Several cases, including one in Texas highly followed by the press, involved companies that created false profits to maintain or increase reported company earnings. Because of the higher apparent net income, the value of the company stock, which the perpetrators owned, would increase, as would management bonuses. For a while they fooled external auditors and Wall Street investment firms that the false premises were true or in some cases got such auditors involved so the schemes would continue working. The failure of several very large companies resulted in several corporate executives going to prison. The failure also cost stockholders dearly and hurt the many salaried employees whose benefits were tied to the company stock. Many lost their jobs as well as large portions of their retirement benefits.

Government payouts were often the source for thievery. Some people who were able to work instead connived to receive unemployment, disability, and welfare checks from local, state, and federal agencies. Since welfare payments were higher for single moms than for families, many unnecessary family splits also came about. At the same time a federal program for retirees and disabled people called Social Security was being defrauded. Many of the payees were dead or fictitious. It also appears that both individuals and businesses cheated the government on taxes due. Both the income tax system (common then at the federal level and in many states and some cities) and the sales/excise tax system (on most goods and services) were being defrauded by false data and statements. I saw one formal opinion that with false benefit payments going out and cheaters paying less in, the US government was losing over 30 percent of its entitled net dollar flow each year.

The government was also paying money unnecessarily to many suppliers and contractors who were not delivering according to specifications or who were overcharging. Many unneeded projects were funded because lobbyists for businesses that provided goods and services to the government convinced officials to support projects of little merit. These businesses used cash bribes, equivalent favors, or, more subtly, reelection contributions to influence government and military purchasing employees to buy and pay for things the people of the country did not really need. Also, there were many court-required payoffs on successful legal suits against all levels of the government. Even when the government seemed victorious, the cost of defending such suits still proved to be a major drain of money. In the end, all these unnecessary governmental expenses added to the burden on current taxpayers and contributed to the deficits that added to the related debt that citizens of the future would be obligated to repay.

There were also rewards in the economy to compensate individuals who were willing to make false individual or property damage insurance claims in order to enrich themselves. Insurance companies, who used paid-in insurance premiums to provide compensation for many kinds of realized risks, were often hit by false or greatly exaggerated claims. These included some paid-off claims for accidents that were intentionally set up, like false rear-ending accidents in the unsafe cars of that day. The people involved in these "accidents" might claim neck injury or back trauma, allowing for legal suits on both medical and property damage grounds. More-significant incidents, such as medical malpractice suits, often resulted in large claims for "pain and suffering" that far exceeded the medical costs themselves. Of course, some of these claims were justified, but the false claims got so bad that many states began limiting the maximum amount that could be awarded for pain and suffering to keep down insurance costs for their constituents. In much of the US, insurance costs for medical practitioners became so high that some doctors began leaving the profession, and others limited or quit private practice. For the insurance companies it was often cheaper to pay off false or undocumented claims rather than contest them in the legal process. The cost of these payoffs, of course, was used as justification to increase future insurance premiums for companies and individual consumers. So the insurance companies did not suffer long from losing these bouts with injury lawyers and their clients.

At some point lawyers changed long-standing practices and began publicly advertising their services for suing on behalf of their clients. I read that such lawyers were called "ambulance chasers." Many law firms in the US solicited clients and initiated large individual and "class action" suits against the government and corporations. They often pursued claims for repetitive small offenses or business mistakes on behalf of a very large number of "damaged" clients. Although many claims were legally justified and the payoffs to individuals could be large, such as the long-standing "asbestosis" cases, it was more common for the suing parties to get very small individual compensation for their claims, while the lawyers received a significant percentage of the very large total. At that time the US had over ten times the lawyers per capita than the next-closest country in the world.

What a host of problems for people and government then! It is a miracle that the government was able to change this interwoven system, even in the seventy-plus years since Pops gathered this information! I think a major factor was that with effective law enforcement, violent and white-collar crime became no longer worth the risk. In our era most everyone can have "enough" of what they want, and most know that the great advancements in law enforcement mean the risk of perpetrating crime is not worth any potential gain. Even before these advancements were fully achieved, when addictive drugs, the underlying source of much of the crime, came under total and strict federal government control, much related criminal activity diminished. Other illegal activities, such as prostitution and sex trafficking, were also subdued by government control even before the basic needs for them were overcome by modern education and the scientific counseling we now enjoy. Essentially complete success came from the combination of highly successful systems for early detection of criminal action, even the human tendencies toward them, so preventative and corrective action could be taken on individuals before anyone got into serious criminal activity. Certainly, the required daily visits with our automated psychotherapists have a lot to do with helping us moderate our desires and avoid crime and violence. I also think our standard prescriptions and the medication discipline we now follow is a big part of the solution.

CHAPTER 13

RACE ISSUES

Andrew:

Some of this material is sure to surprise you. It did me.

It is rather amazing how skin color and country of origin affected people's attitudes toward each other during earlier US history. The physical separation and stigmatization of one hundred years ago just doesn't seem American, but that is the way it was! Race relations seemed to have a significant impact on many issues discussed earlier, including families, education, drugs, crime, and even medicine. Overcoming racial separation and the problems it caused was a gradual process. Even though historical laws were changed and new ones written to prevent prejudicial behavior based on race, actual behavior changed more slowly, only by generational change, it seems to me. Over the four generations since the turn of the century, much of the physical differences between races have melted away, continuing the United States' reputation as the "melting pot" of the world. Even the impact of continued significant immigration to our country has been handled in such a way to ensure much better assimilation.

In the most obvious case of problematic racial differences, the communities of descendants from "colored" slaves, predominantly black Africans imported in the 1700s to mid-1800s, were kept separate, and many life activities were segregated, particularly in Southern states. Slavery had been legally outlawed after much acrimonious debate that led to a very costly Civil War between the states in the 1860s. More Americans died in that conflict than in any other war in which the US participated, including

World War II. The military success of the North accomplished national abolishment of slavery but did not solve racial problems on the human side. Severe discrimination continued even after national law desegregated public schools around the mid-twentieth century.

Millions moved to the US from the Latin sections of the hemisphere, the majority of them illegally. Their skin was browner, their hair darker, and their language different, and they were not fully accepted into society in all sections of the USA for many years. It wasn't until the second decade of the twenty-first century that there was a mechanism for most of those that had immigrated illegally to remain in the US. There was also a lot of movement, predominately legal, by poorer nationals into the US that raised the same sort of issues and informal discrimination. Although racial discrimination was illegal, it was a long time before personal discrimination really ceased.

The inclusion process was far from easy for blacks. Full integration required many additional laws and federal enforcement. Despite blacks already being full US citizens, it wasn't until the last three decades of the twentieth century that real progress was made. Many lives were lost before equality was accomplished. During heated times, there were many marches, demonstrations, and sit-ins in segregated restaurants and other public facilities. There were strong-arm incidents, beatings, and even killings, many of which were perpetrated by the Ku Klux Klan, a violence-prone anti-integration society centered in the Deep South. Most, but not all, of the violence had ended by the century's turn. The economic status shifts, however, were slower in coming. Today, after four generations of increasing racial acceptance and decreasing physical differences, we see few remnants of the problem. A lot of the marital and family blending that has occurred has obviously diminished the problem.

The immigration issue seemed to have involved less public trauma. Most of the problems and differences of opinions that arose had to do with the millions that had illegally crossed the US's borders and did not have anything like the rights of citizenship, including minimum wage, the right to work, employee benefits, or even the ability to be legal drivers of mobile vehicles. Latin communities tended to successfully establish separate communities with little desire to integrate. Most states asked no questions regarding rights to attend school, deeming it better to have educated illegal immigrants rather than uneducated ones. Many state school systems taught the first few years in Spanish to facilitate long-term integration of the Latin youngsters. Of course, the offspring who were born in the US were full citizens with all citizenship rights. But this only added to the problems of deporting the illegal parents if they were caught. Little effort was put into finding and deporting illegal aliens unless they were involved in criminal activity, and for a while there were even big differences in that area between some states and cities.

The concern over immigration issues grew to a critical stage in the fifteen years after the start of the twentieth century. Legal immigration allowed temporary permissions for seasonal workers and those coming into the US for education. Individuals extending their legal stays proved difficult to restrict. Beyond this, illegal immigrants, crossing principally at the border with Mexico, came from many Latin American and other countries. This illegal immigration had been a problem, particularly for the border states, for many years. At the turn to this century, there were an estimated twelve million immigrants in the shadows without legal access to jobs. They obviously found people or companies that would hire them at substandard wages in order to reap monetary advantage. The border states saw the worst of the problem and complained the most. For example, they complained about the cost of lost jobs and about paying the bill for the free public schooling offered to all children, as well as the cost of new citizens when illegal aliens bore their children in the US. There also appeared to be a significant connection between immigration and increases in crime, particularly drug smuggling, prostitution, robberies, and family violence. Many criminal gangs were made up of or organized by illegal aliens.

A national immigration police force tried to maintain legal border crossings, but illegal crossings at other places along the long southern border were very common. There seemed little success in apprehending those who crossed illegally into Texas, New Mexico, Arizona, and California and then gradually moved north and eventually spread across the entire US. Theoretically this was a *national* enforcement problem since border security and immigration was a responsibility of the US federal government. The states seeing the worst of the illegal immigration problem pushed harder for federal enforcement because at the time they bore most of the costs. Some initiated their own border security systems to enhance such safeguarding. After pushing those caught through state courts and the penal system, the states usually turned lawbreakers over to the US Immigration Service for deportation. The states' contention was that the poor performance of federal border control was costing the states themselves for the crimes, the legal proceedings, and the related prison incarcerations.

This issue came to a head when most of the border states, not satisfied by the federal government's border protection, began to require identification showing proof of citizenship. At first, lawmen asked for such identification from people who were likely involved in other illegal behavior. In the late stages, when crime, especially the smuggling of drugs and of illegal immigrants themselves, grew more prevalent, officers with just the suspicion that an individual was not a citizen could ask for ID and make an arrest if the person could not prove his or her citizenship or show that he or she was legally allowed in the US. When terrorism and the threat of it grew, fear of border-crossing terrorists further heightened the demand that our borders be strictly controlled, although this was not to be inexpensive.

Today the situation is dramatically different. Immigration is very tightly controlled, with the borders sealed much better. The main control, however, is that in the US, individuals can do practically nothing without a correctly implanted IDI. Every person's IDI as well as other automatically detectable observation data, such as eye and face patterns or fingerprints, are transparently checked at every building or park entrance and at all transaction points. People without an appropriate IDI or with nonmatching physical attributes are automatically denied further movement and immediately arrested. Improper, false, or duplicate IDIs are easily detected at these checkpoints, where every entrant's IDI can be matched for unique DNA, blood type, and other physical attributes against the nationally maintained database. The IDI system instantly reveals any duplication and falsification.

Today noncitizen seasonal workers and more-permanent foreign laborers are only allowed into the country through special foreign firms contracting with the government. These laborers live in special housing and are well taken care of by government-approved companies. They get special IDIs limited to where they can go. They are basically employees of labor-supplying companies that can be temporarily rented out where there is a legal demand. Visitors to the US also receive temporary IDIs containing all the standard information including their visa timing and the locations they can go. They can be tracked via these IDIs just like the rest of us are and can do nothing without them.

There may be a few leaks and some falsification in this system, but these issues have been proved to be very limited and harsh punishment follows for all caught trying to circumvent the system.

CHAPTER 14

TERRORISM AND WARS

Dear Andrew,

Active terrorism by foreigners started in the 1990s, with attacks against the World Trade Center, military housing in Lebanon, embassies in Kenya and other world centers, and the USS *Cole*, for example. Terrorism seemed to hit a peak with the New York City and Washington, DC, commercial flight incidents on September 11, 2001, but threats and attempts continued afterward, including an airplane shoe bomber in 2009 and then an airplane underwear bomber on Christmas Day 2010. US special forces killed Osama bin Laden on May 2, 2011, scoring one for the good guys. US antiterrorism efforts were beefed up considerably, including unprecedented surveillance, observation, and monitoring of citizens and aliens in the US. Airport security was increased considerably (at high cost and causing major delays and passenger privacy problems). There were copycat terrorism attempts as well, usually by young people, who were not always related to a foreign group. No good solution was seen.

Many countries, particularly but not exclusively in Africa and the Middle East, became more and more out of control as their governments could not maintain centralized leadership. Strong dictators had as much trouble as new democracies. Many of these countries and regimes harbored terrorist activities that included the training and indoctrination of individuals willing to sacrifice their own lives to kill their perceived enemies and sometimes apparently just to attract attention to their cause. Most of this activity was carried out by extremist Muslims who could be easily influenced by independent renegade imams. Much of the suicide bomber activity, although widespread geographically, was directed at the US and Israel and their perceived allies. Some individual renegades even attacked US military bases and were responsible for a huge loss of lives.

It is interesting that in those days there were also many acts of terrorism that were more local. Teens and college students that felt they did not get proper attention or support chose to attack fellow students at their own schools. Individuals who had been fired from their jobs or recently divorced committed murder out of frustration or hate. Some renegade organizations promoted acts of violence, as did individuals who wanted attention or who were mentally unstable. There were gangs whose final induction for new members required killing someone, usually a total stranger. Luckily these local cases are rare today partly because of the advancements in our medical practices related to mental health but mostly due to our very effective surveillance system.

As you know, we only occasionally hear about some terrorist act being tried in our country today, but certainly they are more frequent around the world. However, the level of activity was strikingly different to the point of becoming unbearable soon after the turn to the twenty-first century. Such acts were usually carried out by individuals or small groups trying to publicize or call attention to their causes. In cases where deaths resulted, the acts were often at the cost of the terrorists' own lives, whether that meant them living their days out in prison or dying in the terror act itself or at the hands of law enforcement. Many acts of terror seemed to be a way to get publicity for a strongly felt cause. Many were seemingly random to draw attention to the perpetrators themselves, often via their own suicide. Some spouses or ex-spouses, whether abandoned or a perpetrator of or victim of mistreatment and abuse, became mass murderers by the way they carried out retribution.

There are many examples of copycat terror acts tracing back to the early years of our republic. The acts in our history books related to the US revolution to gain independence from England can be thought of as terrorism even though we attribute much good to the results today. Clearer examples of terror acts are the presidential assassinations and attempts. Abraham Lincoln's assassination at the hand of a slave state rebel is one of the most well-known, but there were many attempts on US presidents' lives.

Although some attempts were politically motivated, most were attributed to people with mental illnesses. Assassination attempts continued to be a concern, and it was common for well-known public figures and show business personalities to have bodyguards or the equivalent to protect them from harm at the hands of others.

There were also many terrorist-type acts in the early days of unionization of industry, usually resulting in the destruction of property, although beatings and even killings occurred when people crossed picket lines. Through the years there have also been individuals mentally sick enough to cause death and destruction. Some viewed their actions as justified because of some ill done to them and harbored in their mind. Others seemed to view the terror acts as a challenge and wanted to see if they could get away with it. The terror acts ranged from aggressive or intoxicated teenagers causing property damage to those terroristic individuals who mailed bombs or contact poisons to their victims. There were several highly publicized cases where individuals tainted on-the-shelf products at food stores with the intent to harm those using the products. Some planted hard-to-detect bombs in normal-looking packages that they left on doorsteps or mailed through delivery services.

From 1990 to 2015, terrorist acts took many new turns, ranging from high school students who carried out careful plans to shoot classmates who had taunted or embarrassed them to disgruntled employees who shot up fellow workers and other forms of outcasts trying to get even with the world. Some used sniper tactics to kill people they didn't even know. Some that opposed abortion chose to kill doctors that performed these procedures. Such acts escalated into the bombing of buildings to show opposition to some other things companies or governmental agencies were doing.

The height of terrorism coincided with the rise of radical Islamists, who seemed to have two targets. One target area was Western countries where moral standards had declined considerably and whose media depicting that decline was spread through the greatly expanding communications capabilities of television and the internet. The United States' support of Israel, the wars against Iraq's and Afghanistan's extremist regimes, and later the action against Iran nuclear facilities were also instrumental to making the US a target. US support in the Middle East did not always appear consistent. Sometimes the US supported extremist Muslims seeking to overthrow royalty or other long-term leaders who ruled and controlled the military in many of the oil-rich Islamic countries.

The acts of terrorism in western European countries and in the US took many forms, such as the airplane hijackings and attempts to destroy public transportation facilities, including train and subway systems. Bold terrorist moves in other places in the world, such as Australia, were highly publicized, as were terrorist events in the Middle East and eastern Africa. In these areas, the acts were mostly directed against the US and United Nations military located there.

However, nothing had the impact of the simultaneous hijacking of four commercial airline passenger jets in September 2001. Two of these jets hit and brought down the two largest office buildings in New York City, killing thousands. The second hit was seen live on TV by many Americans. Another jet hit the US military headquarters, the Pentagon, in Washington, DC. The fourth plane was destined for Washington, DC, as well and was possibly headed for the White House, the capitol and the US president's home. After hearing on their cell phones what had happened in New York and Washington, the passengers took matters into their own hands and made the personal sacrifice of their lives in order to prevent a bigger disaster. They successfully struggled and overcame the hijackers, and the plane ultimately crashed in an open field in Pennsylvania.

For some time, there were many other attempts at various forms of terrorism from mass poisoning and industrial and utility sabotage to other bombings. Radical Islamists that were part of the US military, for example, successfully attacked and killed many soldiers at American bases, including several in the US proper. Others acts of terror were partly successful but soon mostly thwarted by the quickly enacted program that got the national ID program going. Only when the government, with the approval and cooperation of the American people, acquired the capability to know where every individual in the US was at any time did the threat of terrorism significantly decline. Later, when the knowledge of the mental state of each person in this country was possible, acts of terrorism essentially disappeared.

CHAPTER 15

WORLD SITUATION

Andrew:

Much of this you know about or has been mentioned before, but I will try to be more thorough here. During the years our ancestor produced the documents we found, the major economies (US, Europe, Japan) faced new problems and challenges. The eurozone had financial problems largely caused by financial diversity among the inhabitants, particularly the non-citizens. Growth economies like China, India, and Brazil were booming, although China's growth slowed. Old USSR countries, including Russia itself, struggled with major growth and control issues. Canada, Australia, and New Zealand seemed to be doing fine.

There were major uprisings in Arab/Muslim countries. Some had been ruled by tough dictatorships, like Egypt, Libya, Syria, and even to some extent Tunisia. Israel had a special security situation and often unique solutions, which they thought necessary, due to the animosity of neighboring countries. Wars remained in progress in many places, including Iraq, which had overthrown a tyrant who had threatened the area's peace and taken military action against his neighbors. A time period that became known as the Arab Spring saw many changes in that area, all at the same time.

Even the Philippines had problems and had to deal very harshly with its terrorist activity. In Central and South America corruption was clearly apparent, including at the highest levels. This was often related to drug trafficking.

The situation in the rest of the world was not very favorable to the US shortly after the turn to the twenty-first century. The US, theoretically in defense of freedom, had two official wars in progress and was involved in military or covert action in many other countries. For a long time after the end of World War II we had many overseas military bases, and we also militarily supported many regimes to try to maintain a more peaceful status quo in the world.

The US was also by far the largest foreign aid provider in the world. Like today, there were frequent shorter-term natural calamities, such as drought, major onshore and ocean-driven storms, earthquakes, and volcanic eruptions, that strained the citizens and the governments of many countries. There were also political regimes that enriched themselves and their friends to the physical and economic detriment of the people they ruled. The US government and American-based nonprofits often stepped in financially to help but also frequently stepped in militarily. Some US citizens saw helping the poor and our allies in these and other countries as a major economic drain, although these government expenditures, percentagewise, were not that large compared to the total government expenses. Some of these same countries did become major suppliers of raw materials and also manufactured goods, with their cheaper labor displacing US companies and many homeland jobs. The issue of international poverty became better known and publicized as people realized its extent and its terrible impact on human lives. Nonprofit organizations and public figures, including show business celebrities, did much to make the public aware of how extensive and bad the situation really was in a large part of Africa and some parts of India.

Some of the unfavorable trends in the world were very long term but still influenced the then current US economy negatively. Life span increases more than offset somewhat declining birth rates, and for many years the growing world population put enormous pressure on world resources and the escalating cost of developing them. Natural resource development exceeded what many thought could be sustainable long term. Foodstuffs, for example, were developed by destroying natural areas. In the Amazon basin, larger and larger percentages of the natural wilderness were converted to edible crops such as soybeans and corn. Incidentally, these crops produced much less oxygen per hectare than the natural forest.

US companies were in the forefront of developing seeds and agrichemicals to produce foodstuffs that had higher yields and that were less susceptible to damage from disease and insects. These developments helped to cover part of the growing demand but by no means all. Acreage growth had to continue to achieve balance between world population and food production. Advancements in nutritional knowledge helped in some cases but required more resources in others.

Commercial fishing and whaling came under heavy pressure from environmental groups as scientists were better able to determine population changes in all forms of sea life as well as the potential threats of extinction. In many remote mining developments, the environmental destruction was apparent but not widely publicized. Great wilderness areas were converted to large fields of mine spoils, destroying the natural beauty and changing the environmental balance. Waste disposal became a major economic and environmental concern in remote areas, such as in mining, but also in metropolitan areas from burning trash and destroying other waste products. All these environmental subjects became important political issues as more-extensive scientific data regarding related harmful effects was developed and widely understood.

The US citizenry found itself on both sides of many of these issues. Some industrialists supported an almost "anything goes" business-growth attitude along with others, including many individual citizens, who were willing to let the development happen as long as it was "not in my backyard." International and US conservationists, on the other hand, fought to prevent such activities, in some cases risking their lives. For example, some did lose their lives trying to deter whaling ships at sea. Many became actively concerned with the long-term effects that industrial, commercial, and individual practices would have on the earth's basic resources like air and water as well as on the earth's temperature. Both sides spent heavily on research and on advertising promotions to sell their views. The investigations, unnecessary developments, and conflicted spending on these emotion-riddled activities were clearly counterproductive to the economy. A more evenhanded approach to such studies with much less competitive rhetoric and promotional expenditure was finally recognized as needed by the mid-twenty-first century, and appropriate legislative controls were implemented.

In the news every day in those years were struggles with terrorism and threats of terrorism both in the US and against US interests and investments abroad. I covered the problems with terrorism itself previously. Suffice it to say that the bold attacks against military and industrial personnel and installations were often in the news and were very bad for the national morale. Such publicity diminished the United States' will to continue supporting more-distant countries and regimes, particularly in areas where it was unclear whether they even wanted or needed our presence. Although the breakdown of the USSR in the 1980s relieved pressure and many expenses from the "Cold War", as it was often referred to by Sir Winston Churchill, the US spent many billions of dollars to ensure the success of the breakaway countries.

Meanwhile, some other powerful dictatorial regimes threatened neighbors who were friendly to the US. Some apparently acquired the ability to deliver nuclear bombs. Countries previously considered renegades, even longterm holdouts like North Korea, finally took their places among the US, Russia, China, India, Pakistan, and the established western European nuclear powers. Iran, at this time, supported terrorism in Europe and the US, created many problems in the Middle East for the US and its allies, and surreptitiously developed nuclear weapons under the guise of producing nuclear fuels for power usage.

Not including the costs of our overseas military and military support for allies and against terrorist regimes, US exports of technology and foodstuffs were large but easily exceeded, in financial terms, by imports, largely manufactured goods. In those days a very large amount of US individual and corporate tax receipts went to support the economies of other places in the world. Despite the already large national debt and the interest charges that accompanied it, for a long time the Washington politicians chose to add additional debt in order to continue these foreign expenditures as well as to continue paying an increasing amount for the cost of running the government, the military, and the welfare system of the US. For a little while monetary policy enabled the country to keep interest rates at historic lows, but inflation could not be forestalled. With the recognition of this inflation came higher interest rates leading to much-higher interest costs on the increasing government debt. To many, this approach appeared to be a one-way path to economic destruction.

Knowledgeable Americans saw that this strategy could not continue and began to insist on changes that would not inflate them into poverty or mortgage the futures of their children and grandchildren. It was time for some drastic changes.

CHAPTER 16

COMBATING CRIME—LAW ENFORCEMENT

Andrew:

Our law enforcement system of today is much smaller and more efficient than in prior times. In our ancestor's day there were many levels of police and other enforcement officers, with many them on the streets. The extent of criminal activity was much, much larger, such that even with a large enforcement community, crime was still not adequately controlled. The law enforcement systems of that day were divided geographically and had many hierarchal levels and independent functions with relatively poor communication between them.

Criminal activity—the combating of it and dealing with the results of it, including the legal proceedings—was widely publicized in the news media. Originally this was justified because of the expected crime-deterrence effect. The publicity proved not very effective in reducing criminal activity. There were even copycat criminals who were influenced by what they read and proceeded to try the same thing. There were also part-time criminals who held regular jobs or were students and supplemented their income through petty thievery and even armed robbery. Many crimes were never detected, and others were improperly prosecuted, resulting in justice not being served. Many criminals who were caught and found guilty by the courts received punishments that seemed light relative to the crime. Worse yet was that most criminal lawbreakers who were caught, sentenced, and interred became repeat criminals because the rehabilitation process was so poor.

Law enforcement also became very dangerous during these times. The easy availability of deadly weapons, largely through the broadening of legal private gun ownership, increased the risk associated with police activities. More and more sophisticated arms were too easily available, many through entirely legal sources. It became common for even small-time thieves to carry firearms, particularly pistols, and be willing to use them. The entertainment industry had familiarized the public with gun use and to some degree glamorized criminal activity and made light of the consequences of using deadly force. Ordinary citizens fearing for their own safety called for easier availability of handguns and even military-style weapons and then armed themselves and got related training for protection. This greater abundance of deadly weapons led to more injuries and deaths from accidental firings and from the consequences of intensified arguments and disagreements. So, shooting injuries and deaths subsequently grew. I would not say that crime became more acceptable, but the consequences did become deadlier as well as more widespread.

Although the science of crime detection was rapidly improving during those years, the law enforcement agencies' task became harder and harder because of several factors. The intensity, sophistication, and sheer volume of criminal activity grew faster than the city, county, state, and federal institutions could afford to add appropriately trained personnel. Poor economic conditions during some of this period and the resulting lower-than-expected tax revenues did not help. Inadequate capacity for incarceration also meant many criminals were given early parole or shortened sentences. This put known criminals back on the street. Prevention of crime became more and more difficult, often bordering on the impossible. Instead, almost all the resources were allocated to the follow-up activities: determining who and where the criminals were, finding them, making arrests, imprisoning those arrested, and coordinating with the court system to handle judgment and incarceration requirements. It must have been terribly frustrating that there was no detectable correlation showing that the level of enforcement effort and money spent reduced the level of criminal activity.

Unfortunately, there were also law enforcement people who themselves were involved in crime or could be bribed to look the other way. There was regular reporting of cases where speeding or other traffic infractions could be overlooked for a small bribe or even a sex act. Prostitutes sometimes avoided arrest by offering their services to police officers. Law enforcement personnel were successfully tempted to improve their financial situation substantially by assisting those involved in illegal activities, particularly in drug trafficking. Although I will summarize the court system situation separately, let me say here that the same sort of thing happened at higher levels of the justice system. Frequent accusations of bribery or favoritism were directed at jury members, prosecutors, and judges, all of whom could impact the severity of punishments as well as decide or influence the degree of innocence or guilt of accused criminals.

CHAPTER 17

LEGAL SYSTEM AND JUSTICE

Dear great-grandson,

The legal and justice systems near the turn of the century were quite different from today. They were much more extensive, elaborate, and complicated, with many difficult problems. Courts to resolve disagreements were needed in every city and town and for several specialty areas and severity levels. There were two basic areas: criminal courts, where guilt and punishment were decided for lawbreakers, and civil courts, where arguments related to family issues, product/pricing issues, or contractual matters were resolved. Many times, criminal and civil matters overlapped. The American justice system required about ten times the lawyers per capita than the world average. Most of the judges in the judicial system were elected, and most, although not all, were trained professionally in law. Essentially all those arguing for clients, whether for criminal or civil cases, were lawyers, although some persons chose to defend themselves. Most all serious disagreements of that day that were investigated wound up in the court system for resolution. Arbitration before legal action became part of most contracts but did little to reduce the number of court cases.

The criminal courts had to decide guilt or innocence of accused lawbreakers. Like today, the jury system tried to ensure fairness in the process. The skill of the court's legal staff and of the defense attorneys clearly affected the outcome of many cases, but so did the capabilities or biases of judges. There were also many cases of evidence destruction, misuse, or fabrication; such mistakes influenced important decisions and sometimes caused bad decisions. Like today, for those found guilty, the court and the juries also had the responsibility to mete out the penalties, which could include monetary fines, prison incarceration, or both. There were of course elaborate laws to follow defining the extent or range of punishment for criminal acts as well as precedents from previous cases to guide these decisions. There were also various levels of appeals, usually in separate courts, where additional hearings or trials concerning issues of uncertainty on guilt versus innocence or concerning the level of punishment could be further judged. Courtroom practices could also be challenged there.

It appears that for many years the criminal courts were stacked up with more cases than they could handle in a timely way. It sometimes took years to get a case to trial and then years to get a final resolution. Dependent on the severity of the crime, the accused could be incarcerated during this waiting period or forced to put up a bond guaranteeing payment to the court system if they disappeared before the trial. Bondsmen provided the bonds for the accused at substantially less than the bond face value, but these bonds also reflected the risk the bondsmen perceived. This practice reduced out-of-pocket costs to the accused but left the bondsmen with the job and expense of finding any accused criminals that disappeared. It is said that their methods were often harsh!

The civil court system dealt with settling arguments between plaintiffs, those parties in disagreement about their obligations to each other. Family matters were settled here, such as who had responsibility for the children in marital divorce cases or when young parents died. Some criminal cases also became civil cases as injured parties sought compensation for their damages. Civil cases required only a majority agreement of the jury to reach a decision, whereas criminal cases then required the jury to reach 100 percent agreement. Sometimes accused parties could be found not guilty of criminal acts but still found guilty in a civil court and forced to pay huge settlements.

Cases about unfair business practices were prolific. In these cases, plaintiffs argued they had been physically or monetarily damaged and sought to get retribution as well as monetary compensation for supposedly illegal practices by a company or an individual. In many of these cases there were class action lawsuits where lawyers represented groups of those physically or monetarily damaged. Some of these class action settlements were quite large, such as the asbestosis and tobacco cases where thousands of individuals sought and received compensation for health problems caused by long-term business practices suddenly deemed illegal. The class action lawyers typically took all their expenses and huge percentage cuts from any rewarded proceeds. In many class action suits, the large number of plaintiffs that had sued had their rewards diluted to insignificance by legal charges.

Success in both criminal defense and lawsuits was of course dependent on the skill of the lawyers involved. Skill was widely dispersed, and the range in costs was very wide between top defense lawyers versus mediocre ones. There was a system for court-appointed lawyers for those who could not afford to pay legal costs. Unfortunately, there were also prominent cases of jury tampering where jurors were secretly paid by defendants to influence court decisions. For many years lawyers' associations did not allow advertising, but it eventually became a common practice, particularly for lawyers seeking to sue on behalf of client groups. Doctors became targets, and legal proceedings against doctors accused of malpractice were common. These lawsuits drove many doctors in private practice to either retire or shift to large corporate health-care organizations if their potential liabilities or insurance costs threatened them financially.

Many of the lawsuits were frivolous with individuals harassing perceived enemies or, more commonly, with individuals or plaintiff groups and their lawyers just seeking money. It was clear that some accidents, especially those involving the then self-operated automobiles, were staged for the expected lawsuit income. Similarly, products were sometimes doctored to create deficiencies, like when a woman once sued a large chain of sandwich shops for a razor blade she had "found" in her burger. Such incidents were frequent, and lawsuit threats were often successful because the accused believed paying out a settlement would cost less than going to court. Any penalties companies incurred as well as any payments they made to plaintiffs of course had to be built into the costs of their offered goods and services, so pricing was adjusted. So, consumers were the ones really paying.

In those days, in both the criminal and civil systems, court operating costs were well beyond the income from fines, penalties, and court costs assessed and paid by guilty parties and losing plaintiffs. This excess had to be carried by the taxpayer. Courts and court proceedings and costs proliferated for many years. The resources required were much higher than those today, largely because there is so much less crime now and far fewer arguments to be settled. Also, guilt or innocence is much more easily resolved now because of our national observation and tracking systems. The number of criminals and therefore crimes is far smaller today because there are much fewer unsatisfied needs and much less disagreement between parties. In addition, the criminals we do have are quickly removed from society. They have their own farms, where I understand they are either cured of the tendency toward criminality or die earlier due to the withholding of the illness-prevention and life-extending medications the rest of us receive.

CHAPTER 18

BUSINESS AND INDUSTRY

Andrew:

It seems extremely difficult to believe now, but sometime prior to about 2020, almost all farming, manufacturing, retail, transportation, and utility enterprises were owned by individuals. Most of the larger enterprises were owned by groups of individuals, usually shareholders of corporations. These corporations had varying degrees of success; many failed. In the manufacturing and marketing world there was a very wide variety of products and services offered to the public. As it is now, of course, transportation of goods from farms and processing and manufacturing facilities to intermediate storage and then to final distribution points was necessary. This transportation took a lot more resources then than today both because of the inefficient vehicles they were using and also because the competitive environment resulted in far less than optimum delivery routes and systems.

The large public companies were managed and staffed at all positions by individuals who were compensated by the corporation. The companies also provided a range of benefits to their employees, such as medical insurance and continued compensation after retirement. These benefits varied considerably between companies. Job changes, voluntary and otherwise, often upset the security of such arrangements. The federal government itself also provided some medical and income plans to cover the cost of postemployment living. One government-funded income plan was called Social Security. Workers paid into this system while employed, and then when they retired, usually between the ages sixty-five to seventy, they received Social Security payments as long as they lived, usually another ten to twenty years at that time. Other related government plans helped support those individuals that were temporarily unemployed as well as a large number of physically and mentally handicapped citizens. The Medicare program, which lasted quite a number of years, supplemented payment of medical services for all Americans.

The real differences between competitive products were often negligible. Many items and services were bought mostly because of advertising and media hype. Companies were driven to increase their profits because increased profits also tended to increase employees' salaries and bonuses as well as ownership profits for stockholders. Volume was important, as was keeping product costs down. Product turnover was increased through product design that often promised more but purposely included less than advertisements seemed to indicate. Many products broke or wore out faster and were expensive or impossible to fix. Lots of companies very intentionally introduced new designs frequently, annually in the case of many technical products, such as personal computers. Companies that tried to compete were often unsuccessful, even if they had better products, because of well-orchestrated actions by their major established competitors. Larger companies often quickly put smaller companies out of business with competitive moves or bought them out.

Apparently, these trends were evident to most consumers, but the general affluence of the population prevented significant protest actions. Even when economic times got worse, the public had little choice but to accept whatever products and services were offered them. Later, when individual incomes for more of the public did not kept pace with the rising prices for the cleverly promoted "needs," the demand for government entitlement programs grew.

Early in this period the then long-existing US stock market for corporate ownership shares became very active. Long-term investors in corporate ownership had fared very well since the pre-1940 Depression that was accompanied by a major bust in the largely unregulated stock market. Then, after the long period of plenty following World War II, the market again became more and more heavily influenced by financial speculators whose only stake was their own profits, which often could be realized whatever the direction of share prices. Some business owners and officers had similar attitudes, emphasizing their own income over that of their stockholders or employees. Significant financial busts occurred. For example, right at the turn to the twenty-first century there was a flurry of interest in emerging technology stocks that got way overblown. Unjustified overpricing and then a severe decline accentuated by heavy stock trading resulted in huge losses for many institutional and private investor groups and financial speculators on the wrong side of these valuation swings. But this was only a preliminary bout compared to stock market action later in that first decade of the new millennium.

Between 2000 and 2015, the US national economy developed very significant problems, as did the eurozone, which included most of the developed countries in western Europe. The source of much of these problems appears to have been selfish missteps by the financial community combined with poor government regulation and overspending. Federal budgets and regulatory law for some years had been driven by politicians whose main aim seemed to be ensuring their own reelection. The more government spending on "pork barrel" projects and other designated favoritism, the more campaign funds and aligned votes came in. The feds on both continents seem to have complicated the situation with ill-considered steps aimed at recovery. In the end, the failure of these attempts necessitated major changes in the way the US national economy was run, changes that still benefit us today.

The US dollar, like the yen today, became the world's exchange currency after World War II, replacing the English pound. However, just half a dozen decades thereafter, greed and poor management in the financial industry and business changed all this for the US as well as for western Europe, the two areas that together had dominated world economics for so long. Special, country-independent currencies were even introduced and became popular with speculators and benefited or hurt investors with their wide swings in value. It is hard today to believe this particular aspect of the financial world was acceptable.

CHAPTER 19

SHIFTS IN THE ECONOMY

Dear Andrew,

The two-term president who took office in 2000 was faced with many difficulties, including the successful terrorist attacks on New York's World Trade Center that completely destroyed two skyscrapers. These attacks led to the US fighting simultaneously in two significant overseas wars, as well as increasing military covert action and intelligence spending, all ostensibly to combat terrorism. These actions were on top of already large expenses for maintaining a military presence around the world. This president also overran federal budgets in order to promote US economic growth, including making large federal tax cuts during these apparently prosperous times. During his eight years in office, these initiatives drove government debt and federal financial exposure much higher.

One aspect of the shifts was the government's encouragement of too much home construction. Home mortgages, many of them guaranteed by semi-governmental agencies, were too easily obtainable, and this encouraged overbuilding, which in turn resulted in home ownership by many who did not really have the financial wherewithal to own a home. By the end of this president's last term, the secondary market in these weak mortgages, predominantly packaged together as high-rated bonds, became overheated and failed, as did the unmonitored market for contract insurance on these bonds. It became clear to all that there had been too much home construction and far too many poor-quality mortgages.

When this situation was fully recognized, a major crash in the mortgage-based bonds and related insurance contracts led many financial firms and financial subsidiaries of other firms to the brink of bankruptcy. Some very prominent companies failed, and others were only saved by bailouts in the form of huge government loans. Such bailouts were even given outside the financial community, for example to two of the three major US automakers. Confidence waned, and most other corporate stock securities followed the downward trajectory. Many fund management firms that were heavily invested and leveraged in related securities failed, or their clients took huge losses. Worse, many long-term homeowners saw their major asset decline significantly in value, with some homes becoming worth less than the mortgage balance. Others, who were more marginal economically, lost their homes back to the lender, creating major problems for them, the mortgage holder, and the home construction business. A major economic recession soon followed with many losing their jobs. Economic growth went negative, and unemployment went to over 10 percent.

The weakened markets also exposed many financial problem areas, including several large Ponzi schemes. Firms hiding investment losses were exposed, as were speculators found to be utilizing illegally obtained inside information to ensure their speculative profits. A lot of individual wealth was severely diminished by these events and the reduction of values that followed, despite government support that allowed many failed companies to stay in business. The government's attempts to control the same financial practices that had brought on these problems were largely unsuccessful. Payroll tax reductions and expanded unemployment payments put more money in consumer pockets at the expense of government income but did not have the expected effect on consumer spending that could have led to economic recovery.

During the next president's two terms, the bailouts, the government expense of expanding the social programs in existence, and the added recession burden of assisting the newly unemployed or underemployed brought on huge additions to the national debt. At this time Congress also passed legislation leading to a major expansion in government-supported health care. The admirable goal of providing good health care to all US citizens was to be gradually implemented but required a very large increase in federal spending.

During this period the government chose to keep interest rates low on US government bonds. Government interest rates were structured so that they served as the base for all other debt instruments. Low interest rates were expected to encourage business growth and to encourage consumers to borrow more and spend more. Low rates would also keep government expenses lower for servicing its mounting debt. However, the lower rates reduced income for many retirees and others partially or fully on fixed income. The attractive rates also had surprisingly little effect on business expansion and job growth. Prominent inflation indices the government used to index payouts to citizens during this period did not count energy or food commodities expenses, so they hid much of the inflation that consumers were actually realizing.

As the government spent more and more in response to the recession, many of the measures for governmental stability suffered. Inflation effects of printing more money were at first subdued by transactions between the Federal Reserve banking system and the US Treasury's issuance of government debt. The Federal Reserve bought enough US Treasury bonds with its reserves to keep interest rates low for several years. This strategy was the equivalent of printing more money, a normal cause of inflation, but was not clearly evident in the statistics or in the eyes of consumers. Neither did it expand money flow or business growth. The situation was further exasperated as the US loaned dollars abroad to prevent a crisis in the European Common Market in which the debts of several their member countries became unmanageable. Then the US debt ratings were lowered due to the size of the total national debt relative to the size of the national economy. At this point, low apparent inflation and the record-low interest rates could not be maintained, so the risk of, or actually the start of, a major US depression become clearly evident.

CHAPTER 20

THINGS GOT TOO BAD

Andrew:

My understanding is that the bad situation in the US just got worse and worse during the second decade of the twenty-first century. Fears about personal safety increased, and the economic wherewithal to improve that situation was not available from local, state, and federal coffers. In fact, the availability of such funds was decreasing during this turbulent period. Living standards decreased for many. In addition to the growth in the number of have-nots, the differences between them and the haves had been growing substantially since the 1970s. This factor started to become a major issue in the early 2000s, although it was masked by general prosperity.

The financial and investment crisis initiated by the disclosure of dubious real estate financing in 2008 heavily influenced local and national elections. The first black US president was elected on expectations of improvements that the electorate desperately wanted to see. But the turnaround was unexpectedly slow, and huge amounts of federal spending and a rapidly increasing national debt were required to hold the ship of state steady.

The numbers of unemployed and those with substandard income grew substantially during the severe recession of the second decade of this century. A very large part of the populace could not reasonably survive without the government handouts they received. Their portion of the costs of running the government had to be absorbed more and more by government borrowing as well as income taxes from the higher-income portion of the workforce and increased corporate taxes. The incentive for successful people to progress financially was diminished by the portion of income taken by taxes. These issues all escalated so that the government could no longer cover the perceived requirements by simply taxing the wealthier citizens and companies more and more. For many at the financial margins it was easier to get on the government dole, find ways to dodge taxes, or turn to profitable illegal activities. US government financial restrictions began to result in lower inflation adjusted federal payments for unemployment, Social Security, and medical-related expenses. Inflation was a painful fact for many on fixed income. It simply did not seem possible for the government to get more income to solve all the problems without taxing the drive out of the independent side.

The economic problems had also led to more and more crime across the country. Though much of the rise in crime was related to the still-growing, habit-forming drug business, crime also grew rapidly in the commercial sector, including the manufacturing, marketing, and financial industries. Moral standards gave way to perceived economic needs—or really wants—across the whole economic strata. Drug use increased substantially. Personal safety became a more and more crucial concern stemming from petty crimes such as burglaries, muggings, and crimes involving personal automobiles. The accentuated financial pressures on a large portion of families, particularly dysfunctional ones, created new criminals. Politically inspired terrorism reached new heights, including threats to public water systems. There was also a significant increase in terroristic events by what appeared to be publicity-seeking or suicidal individuals with no significant cause-related reasons. Examples include multiple deaths from shootings at schools, theaters, and workplaces, including military bases. All these killings brought on both despair to families directly involved and increased fear for safety by those not directly impacted. The increase in crime also brought on heightened demand for government-supplied crime-fighting safeguards, protection, and police units as well as increasing expenditures for the legal system and prison system. There were also increases in US warfare and intelligence expenses due mostly to incidents and threats in unfriendly Muslim countries.

An important indicator of public sentiment at the time was the Occupy

Wall Street (OWS) movement that spread across the US and even to some foreign countries starting in late 2011. OWS started with a group of young protestors that took signs, loudspeakers, and tents to a park near the New York City center for banking and finance. It was clear that they and the other protestors elsewhere were very upset about the situation in the US, particularly the circumstances that had led to the shortage of jobs and to the widening of the economic difference between the haves and the have-nots. At first their demands for change were varied and uncoordinated, and they seemed to have no specific suggestions, just disgruntlements. Some of the protests got out of hand, and confrontations with the police resulted in arrests, injuries, and some deaths. There were accusations that outsiders, perhaps paid or encouraged by authorities, had been the initiators of the rough stuff in order to break up the protests. The movement seemed to go underground in the cold winter that year but later revived in a much more organized way with more-specific demands for spreading the wealth. OWS and similar protesting groups formed and grew each year, becoming active all around the US. These protests turned out to be instrumental in driving not just Wall Street but also Washington toward the changes that eventually followed.

The national government could not continue to use tax policies to take from the rich and support the poor without driving the rich (who were often wealth builders for others also) away from the US. Inflating the currency was one answer—dilute the US's indebtedness, which had been grossly increased from government overspending. However, this strategy had very significant downsides to those many retirees on fixed income derived from government benefits or their own fixed investments. Good economists realized that the only overall satisfactory cure to this situation was increased economic efficiency, where public needs could be met at lower costs. How this could be accomplished was a very difficult question.

For several years the government vigorously sought ways to encourage or force independent corporations and companies to seriously develop these efficiency increases and pass the savings to the consumer in the form of lower prices—a feat competition was no longer accomplishing. Companies emphasized advertising hype and mild product innovations to differentiate themselves from competitors and tried hard to maximize profits to benefit the companies' owners and to some extent their employees. The situation got bad enough that the electorate threw their support to candidates that promised to find a fix to these major problems.

Many years prior to the last decade of the twentieth century the US had improved its citizenry's lifestyles by becoming more efficient in the production of needed goods and services. To a great extent, however, US-produced goods and services were concentrated in higher-technology products. This trend was partly due to American advances in space, automation, computing, and military hardware. Interestingly, the US did remain a major exporter of foodstuffs largely due to scale economics and improvements in the productivity of seeds and yield-enlarging chemicals. So the efficiency growth was driven by technology, and much of the traditional, simpler manufacturing business was displaced by new industry in developing countries. After the turn of the century, however, efficiency improvements alone were not enough to lead to improving the lifestyles of all Americans. A small number of Americans, already very wealthy, saw continued improvement in their wealth and lifestyles, but the vast majority saw diminished real income, higher expenses and a marked reduction in lifestyle.

A series of government-encouraged and sometimes government-sponsored analyses by then-existing private and public study organizations came up with similar views of the dilemma, but few offered meaningful solutions. Most of their suggestions and sometimes demands were oriented toward their sponsor's interests and did not cover the whole waterfront as was really needed for the American economy and people.

However, if the variety of similar products could be limited and the quality improved or life span extended, the general public could spend less to fill a particular need. Also, marketing fewer competitive products and increasing the quantity of those remaining was a proven way to reduce costs. Such products could be produced and sold more cheaply, reducing the cost of satisfying the consumer population. The service industries were less open to such a fix, but technology to automate or reduce the labor-intensive part of these services also promised increased efficiency.

CHAPTER 21

THINGS GOT WORSE, BUT ...

Dear Andrew,

As I noted earlier, the US economy was the envy of the world between World War II and the 2000 millennium. The years of that war and a short period before and after it, pulled the US out of a serious economic depression. In fact, US manufacturing prowess, untouched by any direct military damage in the war, had been enhanced. However, the benefits of this success waned.

For most of the period between 2000 and 2015, despite original good intentions, the government financed an excess of Social Security and related expenditures on a current basis and did not put any excess of incoming funds away for future requirements. Related payments were just another budget item to be covered by current government income or borrowing. After a substantial growth in the proportion of retired people and others receiving benefits, as well as a period of high-cost inflation, the various related tax payments from the working population did not cover all the living and medical expenses of retired beneficiaries. For decent security, individuals had to have exceptional employer retirement benefits or save enough money and make private investments during their working years to cover all their needs in the future.

Such retirement uncertainties combined with employment fluctuations led to a very wide span of financial security, or insecurity, for most Americans. People's expectations were also rising—they wanted more. Advertising to sell the "good life" and communications featuring prominent people using popular products accentuated such desires. Government programs themselves worked to help satisfy these needs and meet ever-increasing demands, but the situation eventually led to outright theft. For example, clever and sometimes desperate people learned to cheat the welfare system by taking advantage of poor government controls of the various social programs. Although in the US we have not seen major cycles in several generations, there were business cycles at this time that threw many Americans out of their jobs, making their situations worse. Government obligations did not seem to cycle but only to compound and continue to grow ever larger.

The total demand for income supplement grew as people started living longer due to medical advancements. It became harder and harder for the business operators and the government to support retirees and others unable to work. Population aging was also impacted by lower birth rates. There was an ever-higher proportion of retired people and a corresponding lower proportion of workers paying occupational and income taxes. The problem was also compounded by the inflation of the cost of living, led by medical costs. Many companies had obligations for future medical and retirement costs that exceeded their expected financial capability, and so they started to cut back these benefits. Companies that failed, which were not uncommon in those days, often reneged on these benefits entirely.

The government naturally felt a need to step in to provide additional support for people. The new programs developed were both expensive and inefficient. Government expenditures to help maintain even a minimum living standard grew rapidly along with all the other increasing costs of government for national and local security, health, and education. The projected government net payout growth was forecasted to add even more to US deficit-spending problems, further threatening the American economy. Tax revenues could not keep up, and the US borrowed heavily to finance the spending the politicians thought necessary and justified.

This pattern had been clear enough already as government debt to citizens and foreign individuals, companies, and governments increased, but the issue had not been considered large enough to create much of an incentive to cure it. Not long after the turn of the century, the problem clearly became more acute. Although the move was very unpopular, for a while government bodies increased corporate and personal taxes to support growing expenditures and to try to decrease the deficit spending. Many of the tax increases did not help or were not very successful. Corporate tax increases only increased the prices of products and services, of course adding to purchase expenditures by the local, state, and national governments as well as citizens. Personal tax increases were very unpopular, heavily influencing the voting in elections. Many politicians campaigned on a platform of no more taxes but usually could not keep their promises.

Inflation and devaluation came in cycles that got ever bigger and bigger. Over most of the years since the middle of the twentieth century, the average standard of living had crept up, but late in the century this average began shifting down. The demand on existing programs for health, unemployment, and disability grew rapidly. Government expenditures were enlarged, sometimes by clever forms of theft. Many who were not eligible for government benefits at all and others who could not really meet the full legal requirements figured out ways to participate in the handouts. Unnecessary medical treatment and the sale of unneeded medications and devices could be arranged to financially benefit both the patient and the doctor or supplier. People cheated to increase their share of other entitlements as well, even having bogus divorces. About 30 percent of the population received "food stamps" to help cover food and household needs. This program was one of those most widely subject to cheating, both by individuals and by smaller stores.

Two back-to-back two-term presidents, the first taking office in 2000, were faced with many difficulties, including increased terrorism and overseas wars, as well as increasing military covert action and intelligence spending, all ostensibly to combat terrorism in the US. Large federal tax cuts during these apparently prosperous times made things worse. These initiatives drove government debt and federal financial exposure much higher.

Any fix could not continue to use tax policies to take from the rich and support the poor without driving the rich (who were often wealth builders for others) away from the US. Inflating the currency had been one answer—dilute the US's indebtedness and lower the interest costs, which had been grossly increased from government overspending.

Good economists realized that the only overall fix was increased economic efficiency, where public needs could be met at lower costs. How this could be accomplished was a very difficult question. Government analyst teams were organized to find opportunities for increasing efficiency. This was where our ancestor and his colleagues figured in. Their studies clearly recognized an overall methodology that could help. Marketing fewer competing products was clearly a way to reduce costs and could be done while still satisfying the consumer population.

CHAPTER 22

THE FIX-IT COMMITTEES

Andrew:

Our ancestor really gets into the act here. Apparently, he was right in the middle of one of the controlling committees, judging from some of the bottommost files that I recently examined among all the rest. As I read it: government analysts finally saw an opportunity for increasing efficiency even though it would take several years to implement.

Newly elected officials, many of whom had been put into office because they promised to find and implement a real solution to the national dilemma, took their first steps. The government organized a series of work groups from businesses and universities, with some government staffers, selecting the best problem solvers in their respective areas. Each group was initially charged with developing a surefire plan in six months that would fix the problems in their area of concern in a period of three to five years. Each group also was to estimate the resources it would take to most quickly implement their plan.

On top of these individual study groups was a separate overriding committee with independent top thinkers as well as practitioners from each area. Judging from his papers, our ancestor must have been part of this group. This group was charged with coordinating between committees, condensing committee results, looking for cost-saving overlaps, and guiding the committees toward compatible final plans. This top committee was responsible for combining all the plans and bringing to the president's council one plan for implementation, which would include priorities, costs, timing, and estimates of effectiveness. When the central committee finally put together these separate plans, it was quickly determined that the total cost of developing solutions in all these areas was far beyond the apparent national capacity to finance them.

So, the study groups were then charged to put together a dynamic second version that was better coordinated with plans from other study teams and that also prioritized steps in the action plans to both reduce the resources and if necessary spread out the time required, without substantially reducing the surety of effectiveness. Technology development needs were to be considered as a way of reducing time and cost.

Despite the urgency and clear priority, plan two was in continual modification for almost a year. The coordinating committee our predecessor served on had to recognize overlap and ensure efficiency and consistency between all areas, hopefully minimizing the cost and time of implementation. All of this was finally completed, but even that answer was not enough. The problem was that even the optimized combination of these plans was clearly not going to be affordable in any realistic terms. A parallel study group formed during the second phase was to determine or at least suggest ways to successfully finance all these changes so needed by the country. The American citizens and businesses were already being taxed so much that there was little incentive to work harder. Inflation was already getting out of hand, so printing more money to cover the costs would further ruin not only the US economy but also quite possibly the economies of many other countries who had large investments in US dollars and US-denominated securities.

Suggested solutions from the financial group took different forms, but always a common element evolved. The US economy had to get much more efficient in order to produce a government surplus that would reduce debt as well as produce needed goods and services at an affordable price for both export and domestic needs. At the same time individuals had to be better able to support acceptable lifestyles. It was deemed unworkable to diminish the wealth of successful families and individuals in order to accomplish the goals. Higher taxation of corporations and other businesses would tend to drive them away from the US, exasperating government taxation revenues. Without a substantial and relatively quick increase in efficiency, Americans would have to accept increased security problems as well as a lower standard of living, with fewer goods and services. None of the study groups could come up with any simple answers. Tax incentives for efficiency improvements reduced government income, and significant changes would be too slow in coming.

There seemed to be only two choices or perhaps a combination of them. The government had to take more direct charge to quickly stimulate business and industry and/or somehow reduce the apparent needs now being voraciously demanded by the American people.

Substantially increasing the efficiency of the economy appeared to be the only realistic option, but extreme automation could not happen quickly and would threaten jobs. The question became how a substantial improvement in efficiency could be successfully achieved.

In the end the solution sounds simple. After much debate and public involvement, the government decided the answer was to promote the development of a new giant company that in turn would acquire all significant companies and industries, both public and private. The new company, although backed by the US government, would use its own securities to do the acquiring, paying attractive prices in cash and bonds. Legislators expected few complaints from the sellers because stockholders that so chose could get a windfall of liquidity, since they could specify their choice between stock or a wide variety of bonds. As promised, the new company did not rapidly change management or employees but instead quickly pushed the US to countrywide full employment.

CHAPTER 23

THE BIG CHANGEOVER

My dear great-grandson:

The only mechanism that seemed plausible was a very dramatic one, and it would only work if a great majority of the American people accepted it. The proposal was for a government-sponsored corporation to buy out all the significant companies in industry and commerce.

The then president, Donald Trump, backed these changes but was unwilling to move forward without a national vote favoring them. So, after much study, the suggested fix was documented for the public and then was approved in a special national election. The resulting consolidation went faster than most expected. Boards of individual companies were mostly very cooperative. They understood that the conditions of the country had to be improved, fast, and that business and industry had to take a major role. They also knew they had to be flexible and cooperative to make the plan work. The wisdom of consolidating to standardize many facets of the new company was clear. So these leaders helped facilitate the creation of centralized industry groups using the top managers of the old separate companies. These leaders also helped to seek efficiencies for the total system instead of just competing for consumer dollars. The population, many desperate for improvement in their lives, overwhelmingly supported the changeover and its particulars.

The changes were successfully implemented and the buyouts paid for by stock in the new combined company and an array of government-guaranteed bonds. All this eventually resulted in substantially improving efficiency by reducing duplication in resource development, manufacturing, transportation, and marketing. Advertising expenses went down fast, and the expected media cost reduction was gigantic. Efficiency went up at unprecedented levels for almost twenty years. The United States even became a large net exporter of manufactured goods and continued large-scale foodstuffs shipping. The cost of living actually decreased for many years, and amazingly, public services and lifestyles got better.

New independent companies could also be formed with proper approvals, so entrepreneurs could realize major financial gain before their privately held companies were folded into the super company. Innovation was further enhanced because of the encouragement of technology centers, many located at universities. These centers worked to improve materials and methods in all phases of delivering the nation's required goods and services. Good new ideas were quickly adopted on a widespread basis. Unemployment, which the plan very clearly targeted, almost immediately approached the zero mark. Jobs were purposely created to meet the flow of young people and immigrants. Also, the government saw to it that individuals were matched to appropriate career paths and, in the short run, specific jobs based on their capabilities and training. Previously unemployed individuals—even many unemployables—were incorporated into wage-earning work. Some new kinds of jobs were created, like the neighborhood monitors who are always there quickly to check on households if people are absent from their duties, don't take their prescriptions, or miss daily sessions with their online psychotherapists.

In the new system all the old government handouts were eliminated, except for the care of severely mentally handicapped persons. Their care was to be fulfilled by one government-owned company. The rest of the population either worked or by choice lived off their personal savings, converted investments, and retirement plans, which retained their full value in the changeover.

Nationalization of industry was not uncommon in many countries around the world. It usually happened because a government needed more money for the poorer citizens or, in many cases, wanted to increase the diminished wealth of the country itself and/or fatten the wallets of government officials. Earlier in the twentieth century, for example, the operations of US and European energy, mining, and utility companies operating in places like South America and the Middle East were taken over by a national company. Compensation for such takeovers was usually well below the true worth, and sometimes it was zero.

Although a huge majority of the US population was solidly behinds this takeover, it was clear that a monetarily unfair form of nationalization would probably not have been peacefully accepted in the US. Prior to the election, ample time was taken for a major effort to educate wealthy Americans as well as the general public. After this education, the solution was overwhelmingly accepted. The have-nots had guaranteed jobs and new security on all fronts. The middle class saw much more security in their lives and in their savings than the chaotic situation rapidly developing because of recession, inflation, and crime. The rich stayed rich but with fewer options to increase their wealth, unless they chose to legally exchange their stock in the new company or their new government bonds for foreign investments.

Elected officials and members of the various study groups formed a central organization to implement the approved plans and to continually present convincing evidence to everyone that their action plan was absolutely necessary and would work. The most recently elected members of Congress, appointed administrators, and hired officials had promised and were expected by the public to come up with the necessary changes to get the US out of the previously unacceptable position and ominous trend. The proposed solution seemed simple to understand, but even those who had devised it expected it might be difficult to achieve.

The new company moved quickly to buy out all the major businesses and industries that had public ownership as well as the vast majority of the large private companies, as well as absorbing all their benefit plans. Companies below $1 million in sales were not bought out, and those below $3 million in sales could appeal to remain private also. The payments to business owners of public companies, including all stockholders, were equivalent to the value of the companies, as determined by pre-downturn stock market values. Similar logic was fairly applied to the private companies. Apparently before the vote to approve the plan was held, many tests, polls, and surveys had predicted that this plan would be more acceptable than the original study groups expected. The pressure for somehow solving the economic problems had become unbearable and very widespread. The companies owned by either employees or investors had seen their company success drop with the dramatic economic cycles, the extremely high tax burden, and the reductions in overall demand. This reduction in success had led to high unemployment, loss of net worth, and sustenance living for many.

With the agreed-to process, company owners and stockholders simply exchanged their stock or ownership portion for a like value of either stock of the new consolidated company or private, government-backed bonds, with maturities spread over as much as fifty years according to the age and needs of the recipient. Returns on these new bonds were fair, escalated with inflation, and they had the highest security level available. Existing companies would not disappear, just have a new single owner. Individual employees could expect more consistency and more job and income security. Part of the overall plan was to restore, or really to create, 100 percent employment, even adding jobs appropriate for the homebound and handicapped, many of whom were previously on government subsidies. The previous industry that manufactured, transported, and sold illegal drugs in the US didn't last long after the changeover and was basically taken over by the government after effective enforcement became fiscally and technically possible.

The plan had many features that appealed to most all employees. Over time, as anticipated corporate efficiency changes were made on a national scale, it was promised that there would be appropriate job changes and promotions as well as employee movement but with no financial penalty and no danger of being unemployed. Multiple levels of salaries would be maintained with salaries commensurate with responsibility levels and educational, skill, and knowledge requirements. External bodies would review performance relative to requirements and company goals to determine bonuses. Continued opportunity for career growth was part of the promise with a pledge to properly manage the process, maintaining it to be strictly fair and giving rewards to individuals as they deserved. Workweeks were soon shortened because of the large increase in total employment and the efficiency gains resulting from business combinations. We appreciate today that this part of the expectations certainly did come to pass.

Interestingly, in order to pass these laws converting to such a dramatically different business situation and relationship between business and government, an option was included to reverse the process if directed by a national vote, with a specific full-time committee set up at the ready. The situation would not revert exactly to all the previous multiple competitive companies but rather to public ownership of parts of the single corporation that had resulted from the changeover. Companies would again have the rights to split into independent entities, new independent corporations would also be allowed to form, and the full US stock market would be revitalized. However, this repeal option, at least to date, has never come about because the voters have always rejected it in all later elections. Things got very much better in all respects, except perhaps in the area of some personal freedoms. But many Americans believed that the freedom of unobserved movement had been the chief culprit in the country's woes and impending demise. They argued that this freedom had allowed, and perhaps in many cases even encouraged, many to perform illegal or harmful acts in search for profits, booty, or self-aggrandizement.

It appears that the American people as well as the committees were surprised at the quick success of the changeover. Even many of those who had worked on the task forces that defined the changes could hardly believe it. Executives that worked in competing companies were now required to work together with a very clear goal of increased efficiency, and they were provided incentives related to achieving this goal. These former competitors quickly adopted the idea of efficiently and economically providing people what they needed instead of convincing them to want one product over others. Most product and service duplications were eliminated, and most of the advertising previously used to distinguish between similar products was eliminated. The quality of manufactured products was increased so that they would work better and last longer. These products sold well, and the strategy was very successful in reducing the costs of production and delivery.

Unnecessary production lines, plants, warehouses, and transportation segments were weeded out. It turned out, however, that a lot of the expected surplus of capacity was needed to cover the growth of demand. Many Americans could now afford products previously economically inaccessible to them. Extra capacity was also needed to satisfy the realized growth in exports as US goods became both better and cheaper. To ensure continued product quality and capability growth, the new research and development and technology companies were given strong incentives to develop better products as well as new ones. Entrepreneurship was not excluded, since approved new companies under a special government entity were encouraged. The government helped these enterprises by providing operating money and other resources as well as special incentives and longer-term compensation proportional to the success of such new companies.

A special company took over the management of the ensuing shifts in job displacement and manpower requirements. They also worked carefully on assigning personnel to jobs appropriate to their skill levels. This company, which of course still exists today, provides services to optimize placement and enhance skill levels through additional training and schooling. Staffing for positions in this company originally included many former employees of job-placement and recruitment firms, human resources departments, and industrial schools. Besides optimizing placement, this company has the special task of providing training, creating work incentives, and ensuring job satisfaction. Later I think some of that satisfaction was achieved through medications, such as the rumored "happy pill" included in what we take every day.

The government also literally took over the business of entertainment and sports, acquiring all the major general media companies and sports franchises. What we see in our media today is still very entertaining, but it minimizes the portrayal of sex and violence that had become so prevalent. The new megacompany, as owner-operator of all sports franchises, seeks to keep competitiveness between individuals, teams, and locations strong. It also promotes appreciation of excellence rather than just winning. Prices charged for media and live events have been lowered, so more of the public can directly attend or remotely enjoy the entertainment and sporting events as spectators. Expert athletes are still well rewarded, but now their events generate excess revenues to benefit the general welfare of the American public. Sports are no less physical, and injuries still happen, but they do not result from violence between competitors but, as you well know, from accidental falls, overexertion, and strains. The direct-fighting sports have been eliminated or the rules changed so no competitor can purposely injure another one. The emphasis is on skill. I am reminded of sumo wrestling, which was popular in only a few places in the old days but is widespread in the US today and is, I think, the most violent sport now allowed.

Of course, the elimination of poverty and illicit drugs has been markedly successful in reducing violent crimes. Further, the predictable adequacy of income combined with well-thought-out monitoring and control of money and goods has all but eliminated the incentives for white-collar crime. No longer can one hide behind apparent legal entities to steal monetary resources from others. The physical tracking of all individuals, their communications, and their financial resources has severely deterred anyone who wants more than they have from committing criminal as well as hateful acts. The combination of the tracking systems, the national media control, our daily computerized psychological and medical reviews, and our coordinated medical treatments has substantially eliminated crime, violence, and most other threats of personal danger in US society.

CHAPTER 24

REQUIREMENTS AND COSTS
PRESIDENTIAL INVOLVEMENT

Dear Andrew,

Although, as far as I know, our ancestor never met President Donald Trump, it was clear to him that Trump was very involved in much of the process of deciding and implementing the big changeover. The committee did often see Dr. Ben Carson, who was secretary of the interior early in Trump's first term. Whenever Dr. Carson came into one of their meetings, they postponed whatever else was underway to give him an update. Supposedly most of these updates got back to the president, who the committee was regularly assured was following their progress very closely and discussing it in his cabinet meetings.

During his first term Trump followed things closely. It was rumored that he had suggested that the government own the new company but was reminded that that would make it equivalent to Vladimir Putin's approach to communism. The studies and progress on the new approach were well publicized, and early in his second term, Trump accepted a new challenge. He was given the opportunity to leave the presidency and become chairman of the new giant company. He insisted that he could do both, but that option was firmly denied. In addition, Congress would only guarantee him one year of running the new entity, even after much pressure for more time from Trump supporters. Trump accepted these terms, with the stipulation that he could name a successor following his one-year term.

Although my father did not fully document much of the subsequent happenings, his collection of clippings do show that Trump stepped down after 364 days and named Ted Cruz to replace him. Cruz was easily reelected and continued as head of the corporation for many years.

Summarizing, during the early part of the twenty-first century, the US came to a great testing point. Dishonesty at a high level and many, many old political decisions had resulted in an economic downturn and suffering of much of the population. For some time, the perceived demands of the voting population and the influence of Washington lobbyists seeking programs that benefitted their company or industry, including the defense industry, had driven government actions, particularly new spending programs. The long-term consequences of such spending programs were not properly examined. Maybe each program was good, or at least good for part of the population part of the time, but the combination proved to be unaffordable. The major recession in 2008, set off by over speculation in the financial industry, proved to be a major turning point.

At this time of great stress on the economy and most of the populace, the government clearly had no good options. Politicians running for office could point to the lack of success of current officeholders but could not offer cogent alternatives that ensured a workable overall plan. Federal officeholders and agencies tried many angles to stimulate the economy to help the unemployed, underemployed, or underfinanced citizens as well as to generate enough federal tax income to solve at least some of the major difficulties of the times. But neither increasing the handouts to those who were struggling the most or spending federal funds in attempts to improve the economy worked. Mostly these actions increased the federal deficit, about doubling it in the first decade of the twenty-first century. The attempt to hold interest rates low, thereby helping individual borrowers and keeping government financing costs down, used a questionable methodology. The Federal Reserve, manager of the US Treasury and keeper of the currency, in effect loaned money to the federal government by buying large amounts of low-interest Treasury bonds. This strategy was the same as printing more money, and at the same time it mechanically held down mortgage and other interest rates because they were principally indexed to the interest on US bonds. This procedure, borrowing more and keeping interest rates low, would only work if the economy recovered quickly and federal tax income increased accordingly. That did not happen.

The stress on the economy and on individuals got worse during this period, and when the economy started improving, it was too little too late. Although business recovery did start after 2010, the improvements were too slow. Companies were reluctant to expand facilities and operations. Rapid reemployment was not forthcoming, and individual savings were running out, creating even more pressure for additional handouts. To avoid an even-greater recession or a possible depression, the government continually came to the rescue with large expenditures. Federal security ratings were downgraded, and it was only because other world economies were also in recession that the US dollar was able to stay strong relative to other currencies. Even successful developing countries saw their rapid growth diminish as their major customers—advanced economies like the US—suffered because of overspending practices.

CHAPTER 25

SUBSEQUENT DEVELOPMENTS

Andrew:

It is interesting how technical developments supported the new system and helped to create satisfaction in the lives of the great majority of the population.

Identity and location tracking turned out to be helpful for everyone. It is more sophisticated now, but early in the changeover, it was decided and accomplished that every individual would carry a trackable identity device (somewhat equivalent to our IDIs). Now we don't even stop to think about the multiple tiny implants we all carry, but we know we literally can't get anywhere without them. In an earlier time, one of your great-uncles once had one faulty IDI and one that had completely worn out. He knew immediately from his home info center that he had a problem, but he tried to go ahead in his daily routine anyway. He was stopped at the first building he entered. After he passed through the physical-characteristics check station, he was held there until all his related devices were again functional.

I don't even think now about how federal computers track me continuously, but sometimes it is useful if I get lost in a new area, as I can stop anywhere and get immediate help. In the early stages, nonconforming people quickly learned that they had better not be in the wrong place or commit an illicit act, as they were sure to be quickly reprehended. It is just no longer possible to function anywhere while being offline.

Medical and other technical advances have increased convenience as well as safety and security. There is practically no illness compared to the old days. Travel has become completely safe and is cheap compared to prior times. I guess it was not easy for many to give up individual choices on owned vehicles— in those days there were many different kinds of petrol-fueled cars, all requiring a driver. Vehicle choice then was a big deal, and there were many competing manufacturers and marketers. Illegal speeds, carelessness, and substance abuse by controlling drivers caused many deadly and injurious transportation wrecks. That's all changed with the efficient government-owned self-guided cars available anytime and everywhere. It is nice to have safety ensured as we commute and explore our nearby environs. The same is true for more-distant public travel on today's planes, airboats, and high-speed rail. Travel possibilities are much more extensive now, and we can take full advantage of our flexible twenty-five-hour workweek with lots of vacation time to boot. All the automation has made work nothing like it was seventy-five years ago.

One section of our home data center helps ensure we remain healthy both physically and mentally. If something seems out of kilter with an individual, in most cases the MP responsible for that person takes immediate action, either online or personally, as needed. These occasions seem rare now, but earlier, right after the changeover, the monitor jobs were some of the most difficult around. Now, with the daily physical system check and short online counseling session, it is extremely rare that any trouble would be undetected. If something does go even slightly wrong, your monitor person is quick to respond and seek, with you, any help that is needed.

CHAPTER 26

CONCLUSION

So, my dear great-grandson, how do we come down on all this? Is it "What went wrong?" or "What went right?" Is it possible you and I can come to different conclusions and both be correct? I would argue that the government effectively stopped terrorism, crime, and the illegal drug trade; secured citizen health and safety; and greatly improved the economic situation by taking over most of the national commerce, trade, and medical care. These changes enabled our country to solve many of the problems that were increasingly plaguing us around the end of the twentieth century. You could argue that personal freedom and choice became much more limited in this process—the country had to back off somewhat on its goal of being the land of the free. I certainly see your point, although to me we are still free to do what we choose, excepting those things that hurt us, hurt others, or waste resources.

How would you summarize what happened? It appears to me that a lot of people at the turn of the last century were just plain scared for their personal safety and financial security as well as tired of being taken advantage of by less scrupulous fellow citizens. Also, more and more of the prosperous people's income was taken in taxes from all levels of government to combat these tough problems and cover benefit payments to much of the population. We became a nation of givers and receivers, redistributing wealth according to political choices. However, public services and government benefit systems were being reduced. The US economy was just not prosperous enough to pay for all the needs and expectations of most citizens. In those times the government was not fully effective, much less efficient, in taking on more and more responsibilities.

Most of the voting population of 2000 to 2015 had started their adult lives in the boom years subsequent to the Second World War. But around the turn of the century, it was apparent that the lives they'd enjoyed earlier were disappearing. Why? The decrease in comfort level was gradual at first, but with the rapid growth of the societal ills we have investigated in our study, these "I want; I need; I must have … anyway I can get it" problems grew rapidly. Protection and lifestyle maintenance of the populace required more and more effort and expenditures controlled by the elected officials in local, state, and national government, at great cost to the taxpaying public and industry. These government efforts were expensive and usually less than effective. Smart criminals, less-than-honest businesspeople, and governmental officials of all ilk's continued to commit more-desperate acts and find more and more sophisticated ways of continuing to get what they wanted at the expense of others. Many elected officials were part of the problem because of their own greed. Fighting all these problems became very expensive, and yet the enacted solutions then were still far from successful.

As the citizens became more fearful, politicians were finally elected on the promise to correct this mess. These politicians concluded they could only do so or afford to do so by taking over direct control of the economy and many parts of common societal activities. They also took much-stronger positions than previously in security and enforcement. When they determined that there was only one financially feasible way to fix the mess, they took action, and their plan worked. With increased control and enforcement, crime began a rapid demise. Basic economic needs were better met, so there was less reason for illicit behavior. Limited advertising subdued the desire for more and more goods and services, while combining former business competitors and making fewer competing products increased US productive efficiency. Not much later new medical methods, both physical and mental, effectively controlled many desires that were unhealthy or out of reach economically. In some cases, uncooperative citizens were sent to special cities where retraining could be conducted. Basically, our population became more satisfied by both wanting less and having more. The improvement in efficiency of the economy cascaded, and the US regained its position of economic and industrial prominence in the world.

Our lives are much safer now, although I would agree they are a lot more deterministic too. So far there are relatively few who are unwilling to accept this more fixed existence, particularly since the drug and therapy regimes were optimized. As you know, the few misfits sent off to the isolated colonies have much more freedom of choice but must mostly fend for themselves. Taxpayers support nearly all the costs of having these "islands," but this setup of a separate city is a lot cheaper for the government than the previous legal and prison system. Many who go there are cured or corrected and come back to our society after a short stay there. You could say there should be a better answer, but is there?

Considering all these improvements combined with the continued personal challenges of our employment and the related economic welfare we now enjoy, the US is a near-perfect country compared to conditions when my father collected those clippings that got us started on all this.

But I do envy you at your age being able to consider whether there are better solutions or whether eventually people will revolt because they do not have the freedom of choice they would like. Maybe this is a long-term cycle. Your generation could successfully regain more freedom of choice by electing the right people, and then maybe it would be a long time before those inclined to take advantage of this freedom would again threaten the security of others enough to start the cycle all over again. I don't know. You, however, will have eighty years to see for yourself. I guess things could have turned out differently if, early in this century, everyone would have been more honest and fair with others and maybe even have an attitude of helpfulness toward their fellow citizens, but that was just not the situation then.

Good luck.

Your great-grandpop, Pops

CHAPTER 27

TO THE FARM

Andrew:

What happened? I understand you are headed to work at one of the old folks homesteads because of recently discovered activities regarding your use of the pills. I am not sure what this is all about, but I heard that you and some friends found a way to alter the pills to make them less invasive on your thinking. I don't understand either the mechanism or your reasoning, but that's certainly not the only thing I don't understand about young people today. I do hope you can work your way out quickly. I understand this is quite possible and may not take too much effort, mainly just cooperation with officials there.

I will do what I can to see that we are sent to the same farm.

Pops

AUTHOR NOTE

I do not advocate this volume's predicted solution to the problems that are cresting in America in the second decade of the twenty-first century. However, I believe the approach herein may be the only one likely to work, although I hope there are less drastic measures that would solve all the problems. With an education in engineering and business, in my career I worked with large industrial companies and in consulting, predominantly in planning and project development, including work for the federal government. I became aware of corruption and dishonesty at all levels of management in most businesses and organizations I came to know. Sometimes the dishonesty and corruption were in the name of improving performance against competitors but was also often strongly motivated by personal gain, often at the expense of others.

I personally have strived my whole life to be strictly honest and to associate with folks who feel the same way and who also believe an important part of life is to help others. Thank God there are many like us, but we have become outnumbered or perhaps just overpowered by those more ambitious for personal gain and/or less work. The problem is compounded by like-minded associations who aggressively work all the angles to benefit their group, a strategy that usually works against and at the expense of others. The success of the smarter and better-heeled groups takes away resources from the weaker ones, regardless of the merit of either's goals and endeavors. Corruption and dishonesty are rampant and have given competition a bad name.

The solution suggested in this tale leads to full employment—always a decently compensated job for everyone not severely physically or mentally disabled. Any surplus manpower in the system would be offset by reduction in working hours. This approach, accompanied by proper training and work placement for all, with compensation tied to job requirements and thorough but nonthreatening evaluations of individual performance, would help curb ambition-driven dishonesty. However, in my opinion, without moral redevelopment, only the fear and consequences of getting caught will really stop it. Big Brother watching everyone is technically possible and may work, but the total solution herein suggests that professional psychiatry and mind-altering drugs may also be required. Perhaps the latter could ensure happiness and contentment at a lower cost than constant surveillance. Today's question remains, What freedoms must we give up to maintain a rich and productive economy with a comfortable lifestyle for all, when we can't presently count on honesty, fairness, and doing unto others as we would have done unto us?

ADDITIONAL INFORMATION THAT MAY BE USEFUL

SUMMARY

In 2095, while Pops and his college-age great-grandson are cleaning the farmhouse attic, they find a variety of magazines and papers that Pops's father stowed away near 2018. Based on their few hours of examination, they disagree on whether the apparent changes suggested in the papers were all good. Pops agrees to study and summarize what he learns from the documents about the era. Andrew is to return his frank comments. Pops then begins a systematic study to compare this past period against current conditions. He summarizes US conditions in earlier periods in a series of letters to Andrew (the chapters in this book), noting the dramatic changes since then in technology, culture, and economics. Pops is surprised to find just how bad the US situation was during his own childhood. In his investigation, Pops also finds that his father served on a national-level committee that was tasked with suggesting remedies for a then sadly ailing US government and economy.

Pops's study reveals that the startling economic changes from the mid-2010s were not entirely driven by the rapidly advancing technology. The shift back to US prosperity and world economic leadership was accomplished through major changes in the way the economy was structured and run. In a step requiring a national vote, the relationship between government and business was dramatically altered, and the US economy became extremely efficient. The government, after receiving approval in the national vote, made major changes to the way the economy was structured.

As a result, well-paying jobs became available for anyone wanting them or needing to work. Government handouts became limited only to the severely handicapped. Work hours were lessened, and individuals were able to easily find their way toward ideal careers personally suited to them. Recreation time and retirement were secure. Good universal health care became the standard, although it was needed substantially less as the nation's health improved due to medical breakthroughs, healthier lifestyles, more tightly controlled foodstuffs, and tailored standard medications. Personal safety ceased to be a significant concern.

Although the author does not advocate this volume's predicted solution to America's problems, in the author's opinion this approach may be the only one realistically feasible.